new zealand kiwifruit cookbook

jan bilton

irvine holt

Publisher: Irvine Holt Enterprises Ltd
PO Box 28 019 , Remuera
Auckland 1136, New Zealand
©Copyright 1981-1999 Jan Bilton
Cover design Michael Ryan

ISBN 0-9597594-2-5

First edition printed 1981. Reprinted six times.
Japanese edition 1983
Revised edition 1990
Third edition 1999

All rights reserved. No part of this publication may be reproduced, stored in a retrieval system or transmitted in any form or by any means electronic, mechanical, photocopying, recording or otherwise, without the prior permission in writing of the publishers.

Disclaimer: The recipes in this book have been tested by the author. The publisher and author have taken every care to ensure the instructions and measurements are accurate and will not accept liability for injury or loss or damage to property. Photograph – Fruit Sushi page 47.

contents

Foreword 4

Introduction 5

Drinks 6

Starters 9

Mains 17

Salads 36

Sweet Treats 42

Preserves 62

Nutrition 68

Kitchen Help 70

Index 71

The author gratefully acknowledges the encouragement and assistance of ZESPRI International Ltd.

foreword

The unique taste, health-enriching qualities and versatility of New Zealand's ZESPRI™ Kiwifruit make it one of nature's most perfect foods – an eat anywhere, eat any time fruit.

New Zealand is the home of the kiwifruit. Hayward Wright first produced his green-fleshed Hayward variety here in the 1920s, bred naturally from plants brought from China. For 75 years our growers have been perfecting their techniques. And while kiwifruit is now grown all over the world, New Zealand remains the industry leader, marketing high quality fruit globally under the ZESPRI™ Kiwifruit brand.

In 1998 we introduced an exciting new kiwifruit. The result of many years of natural plant selection and breeding, ZESPRI™ GOLD Kiwifruit is the tantalising, golden fleshed cousin of ZESPRI™ GREEN Kiwifruit. This exotic new taste sensation, with its unique, smooth skin and heart of gold, offers hints of melon, peaches and citrus to stimulate the imagination of kiwifruit chefs.

Kiwifruit makes a quick and easy snack – simply cut in half and scoop. ZESPRI™ Kiwifruit is synonymous with putting zest into life and providing essential nutrients, minerals and vitamins needed daily for a healthy diet. ZESPRI™ Kiwifruit is a 'must' in every fruit bowl.

The *New Zealand Kiwifruit Cookbook* brings together a wealth of exciting recipes for both ZESPRI™ GREEN Kiwifruit and ZESPRI™ GOLD Kiwifruit – many of which, I know, will become your favourites. Read, create, eat and enjoy!

Tony Marks
Chief Executive
ZESPRI™ International Ltd.

The New Zealand Kiwifruit Marketing Board is the owner of the brand name ZESPRI™ (as well as other trademarks, trade names, brands and logos) and of all copyright and other Intellectual Property rights associated with that brand.

introduction

Called the fruit phenomenon of the 20th century, the brown-skinned kiwifruit grows on a vine in a similar manner to grapes. In New Zealand, it is harvested from mid-April to early June.

storage

Under the right conditions, kiwifruit will stay firm for six months. The temperature must be kept at 0°C (32°F) and the humidity at 90-95%. Kiwifruit should not be stored with fruits or vegetables which emit ethylene gas as this accelerates the ripening process. Store kiwifruit in the refrigerator to maintain firmness.

ripening

Firm fruit can take from one to four weeks to become soft. To hasten ripening, place the kiwifruit in a plastic bag with an apple or banana – both emit ethylene gas naturally. The fruit will ripen within a few days. It is ready to eat when slightly soft to the touch.

eating

There is little waste in a kiwifruit. The whole fruit, even the skin, can be eaten. Rub the skin gently with a soft cloth to remove any excess fuzz and add to savoury salads. However, the fruit is usually peeled before use.

Where recipes simply specify ZESPRI™ Kiwifruit, either the gold or green varieties can be used. ZESPRI™ GOLD Kiwifruit is virtually fuzz-free and has a distinctive shape.

Kiwifruit are known as 'kiwis' in some countries.

drinks

Puréed kiwifruit can be mixed with a variety of juices to produce interesting combinations. To purée the fruit, mash well with a fork then pass through a sieve.

Alternatively, purée in an electric blender or food processor. Take care not to over-process and crush the seeds. This makes the purée bitter and also spoils the appearance. Process until just smooth then sieve to remove the seeds.

The purée may be sweetened – ½ a teaspoon of sugar per kiwifruit – and stored in the refrigerator for up to three days. A dash of lemon juice maintains the colour.

Slices of kiwifruit can be used as a garnish either on the side of the glass or in the drink.

yoghurt whip

1 large ZESPRI™ Kiwifruit
¾ cup plain yoghurt
¼ cup milk
2 teaspoons honey
2-3 ice cubes

Purée the kiwifruit and sieve if required. Combine with the yoghurt, milk, honey and ice and mix well in a blender or food processor. Serve in a long glass. **Serves 1.**

fruit refresher

2 ZESPRI™ GREEN Kiwifruit
1-2 teaspoons honey
1 cup orange juice

Peel the kiwifruit and purée in a food processor or blender. Sieve if required. Add the honey to sweeten. Pour the orange juice into chilled glasses – with ice if preferred. Spoon the kiwifruit pulp on top and serve. **Serves 2.**

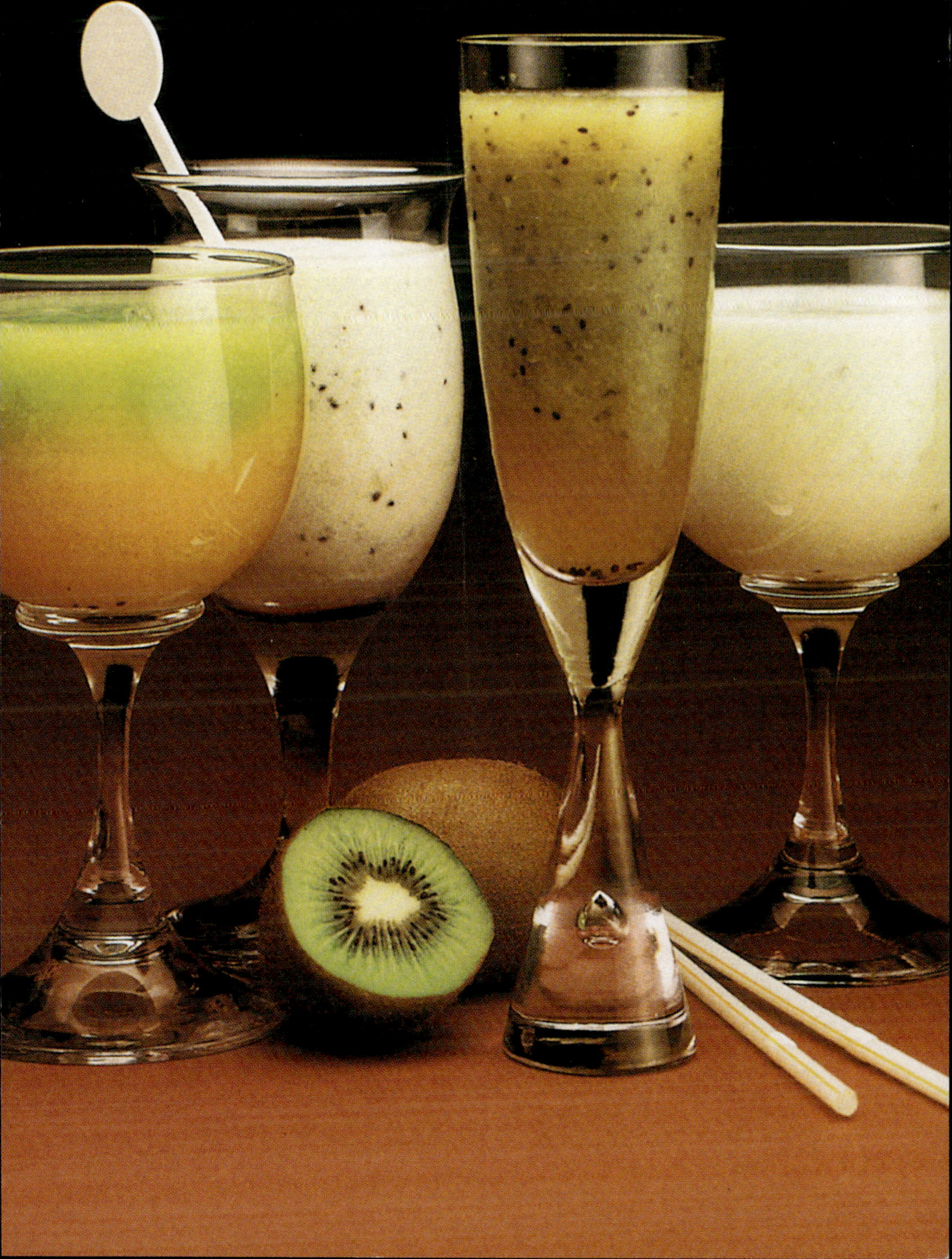

kiwi colada

2 ZESPRI™ Kiwifruit
½ cup each: ice cubes, coconut cream
¼ cup white rum
extra kiwifruit for garnishing

Place the peeled and sliced kiwifruit in a food processor or electric blender. Process for 10 seconds. Add all the other ingredients and purée, until smooth. Do not over-process and crush the kiwifruit seeds. This will make the drink bitter. Pour into chilled glasses and serve. Place a slice of kiwifruit on the side of each glass as a garnish. **Serves 2-3.**

ginger & kiwifruit cocktail

1 ZESPRI™ Kiwifruit
2 tablespoons brandy, optional
¼ cup crushed ice
½ cup chilled ginger ale or ginger beer
kiwifruit and pineapple for garnishing

Place the peeled and sliced kiwifruit in a food processor or blender and process for 10 seconds. Add the other ingredients and purée, until smooth. Pour into a chilled glass and garnish the glass with a slice of kiwifruit or a wedge of pineapple. **Serves 1.**

kiwiberry cooler

2 ZESPRI™ Kiwifruit, peeled and chopped
1 cup strawberries, hulled
½-¾ cup pineapple juice
ice cubes

Place the kiwifruit and strawberries into a food processor or blender with a ½ cup of pineapple juice. Blend until smooth. Strain if desired. Add extra juice if too thick. Pour over ice to serve. **Serves 2-3.**

starters

rolled sushi with kiwifruit

2 cups short grain rice
1½ cups water
2 tablespoons rice vinegar
2 teaspoons sugar
½ teaspoon salt
1 large carrot
3 ZESPRI™ Kiwifruit
3 sheets nori (thin sheets of seaweed)
1 tablespoon grated root ginger

Place the rice and water in a heavy pan. Soak for 1 hour. Cover and bring to the boil, then reduce heat and simmer for 10 minutes.

Remove from the heat and stand for 10 minutes to ensure that the remaining water is absorbed by the rice. Meanwhile, combine the vinegar, sugar and salt then heat, until the sugar dissolves. When the rice is cool, cut the vinegar mixture into the rice.

Peel the carrot and julienne. Steam until just tender. Cool. Peel the kiwifruit and julienne.

Place a sheet of nori on a bamboo mat or clean towel. Spread enough rice over the nori to just cover. Working from side to side, place along the centre of the rice about one third of the carrot, then the kiwifruit. Sprinkle with one teaspoon of the ginger. Lift the mat at one end and form the sushi into a firm roll (like a Swiss roll). Repeat with the remaining nori wrappers. Cut in 2.5 cm (1 in) rounds just before serving. **Makes about 12 rolls.**

finger foods

- Bread cases filled with smoked eel, salmon or tuna combined with cream cheese, topped with quartered kiwifruit slices, sliced black olives and red cocktail onions.
- Sliced kiwifruit on rice crackers, topped with twists of smoked salmon and a sprinkling of caviar or lumpfish roe.
- Slices of kiwifruit on bread croûtons, topped with prawns or shrimps, glazed with aspic and garnished with dill.
- A cube of cheese, a large grape and a ball of kiwifruit, speared with a long toothpick.
- Small pickled mussels, cubes of kiwifruit, and twists of smoked salmon, threaded on small skewers.
- Sliced kiwifruit on a cracker or crostini, topped with a wedge of Brie and a strawberry.
- Small sandwiches filled with kiwifruit and fetta cheese and cut in interesting shapes.
- Crackers or crostini, topped with pâté, sliced kiwifruit and bean sprouts.
- Bread croûtons, topped with kiwifruit and caviar.
- Rounds of bread, topped with salami and kiwifruit.
- Rye bread, topped with salmon mixed with cream cheese, radish and kiwifruit.
- Vol-au-vents, filled with smoked oysters and julienned kiwifruit.

open sandwiches

- Shredded lettuce, ham rolls, mayonnaise and sliced kiwifruit.
- Pickled herrings, diced kiwifruit and onion rings.
- Sliced pork, prunes and sliced kiwifruit.
- Blue cheese, julienned kiwifruit and sieved egg yolk.
- Sliced roast beef, pickled kiwifruit and orange segments.
- Smoked eel, twists of kiwifruit and black olives.

NB *The little black seeds can be used for decoration – they look like black caviar.*

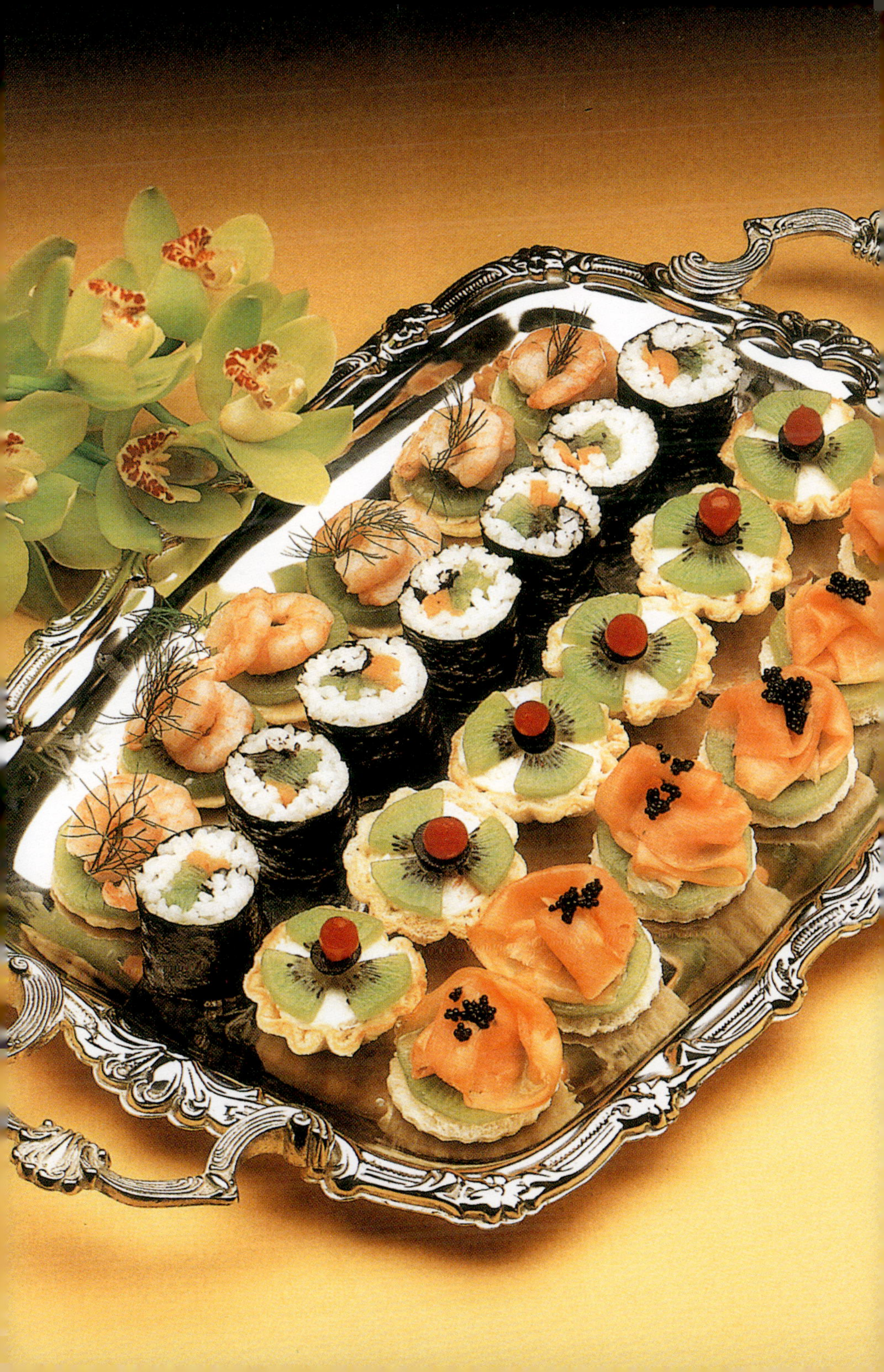

ma ho

Galloping horses – a Thai speciality.

2 tablespoons oil
2 teaspoons each: crushed garlic, ground coriander
250 g (9 oz) lean pork mince
2 tablespoons each: coarsely ground peanuts, fish sauce
¼ teaspoon each: minced chilli, black pepper
¼ cup palm or brown sugar
2 tablespoons chopped, fresh coriander (cilantro) leaves
3 ZESPRI™ Kiwifruit

Heat the oil in a wok or frying pan and stir-fry the garlic and ground coriander in oil, until golden.
　Add the pork, peanuts, fish sauce, chilli, pepper, sugar and coriander leaves and stir-fry until well cooked and dark brown in colour.
　Peel and slice the kiwifruit in 1 cm (½ in) rounds and place on a serving tray. Pile the pork mixture on top of each kiwifruit slice. Serve at room temperature. **Serves about 8.**

kiwi orange soup

1¾ cups orange juice
1 cinnamon stick
4 whole cloves
2.5 cm (1 in) knob root ginger, peeled
¼ cup sugar
750 g (1½ lb) ZESPRI™ GREEN Kiwifruit

garnish: sprigs fresh mint
grated rind 2 lemons

Combine the orange juice, cinnamon stick, cloves, ginger and sugar in a saucepan. Slowly bring to boiling point then cool completely. Strain and discard the spices.
　Peel the kiwifruit, reserving one for garnish. Mash the fruit and rub through a sieve. Alternatively, carefully purée in a blender then sieve to remove the seeds. Stir the pulp into the the juice and refrigerate, until well chilled. To serve, pour into six soup bowls and garnish with sliced kiwifruit, mint and lemon rind. **Serves 6 as a starter.**

whitebait & kiwifruit roulade

Crabmeat or chopped shrimps can be substituted for the whitebait.

225 g (8 oz) New Zealand whitebait (fresh or frozen)
4 eggs, separated
¼ cup cream
salt and pepper to taste
2 tablespoons grated Parmesan cheese
3 firm ZESPRI™ Kiwifruit
200 g (7 oz) cream cheese (at room temperature)

Pre-heat the oven to 200°C (400°F). Wash and drain the whitebait. Pat dry with a paper towel.

Combine the whitebait with the egg yolks, cream, salt, pepper and Parmesan cheese. Beat the egg whites until stiff, then fold one spoonful of the egg whites with the whitebait mixture (use a metal spoon).

Fold in the rest of the egg whites very carefully so the volume is not lost. Pour this mixture into a greased and lined sponge roll tin about 23 x 35 cm (9 x 14 in).

Bake in the oven for 10 minutes. Turn the roulade out onto a cheese-dusted sheet of foil. Cool until the steam has subsided.

Peel the kiwifruit and thinly slice. Beat the cream cheese, until smooth.

Spread the roulade with the cream cheese, then cover with thin slices of kiwifruit. Carefully roll up the roulade, cover entirely in foil and chill well in the refrigerator. To serve, cut the roulade into 1 cm (½ in) slices and serve either as a starter or a main course. **Serves 8.**

kiwifruit & caviar

Kiwifruit halved, scooped out and filled with caviar and prawns.

3 large ZESPRI™ GREEN Kiwifruit
18 large prawns (shrimps)
3 tablespoons black or red caviar or lumpfish roe
salt and pepper to taste

Cut the kiwifruit in half using a zigzag movement. Carefully scoop out the flesh, leaving about 5 mm (¼ in) around the outside edge. Cut the flesh in 5 mm (¼ in) cubes.

Select six cocktail sticks and thread two prawns onto each. Dice the remaining prawns. Mix with the diced kiwifruit, caviar or lumpfish roe and the salt and pepper. Firmly set the kiwifruit shells into six egg cups.

Carefully fill the shells with the combined ingredients. Top with the skewered prawns. Serve on a plate surrounded by tiny squares of buttered rye bread. **Serves 6.**

kiwifruit & grapefruit sorbet

A cooling starter, or alternatively, serve between the main course and dessert as a palate refresher.

¾ cup sugar
2 cups water
zest and juice 1 grapefruit
6 large ZESPRI™ Kiwifruit

Dissolve the sugar in water in a saucepan, add the zest and grapefruit juice and boil steadily for 10 minutes. Chill.

Peel, mash and sieve the kiwifruit. There should be about 2 cups of pulp. Combine the pulp with equal amounts of cold syrup. Freeze in an ice cream machine. Alternatively, freeze in a suitable container in the deep freeze, until mushy. Beat well, then freeze until firm. **Serves 6.**

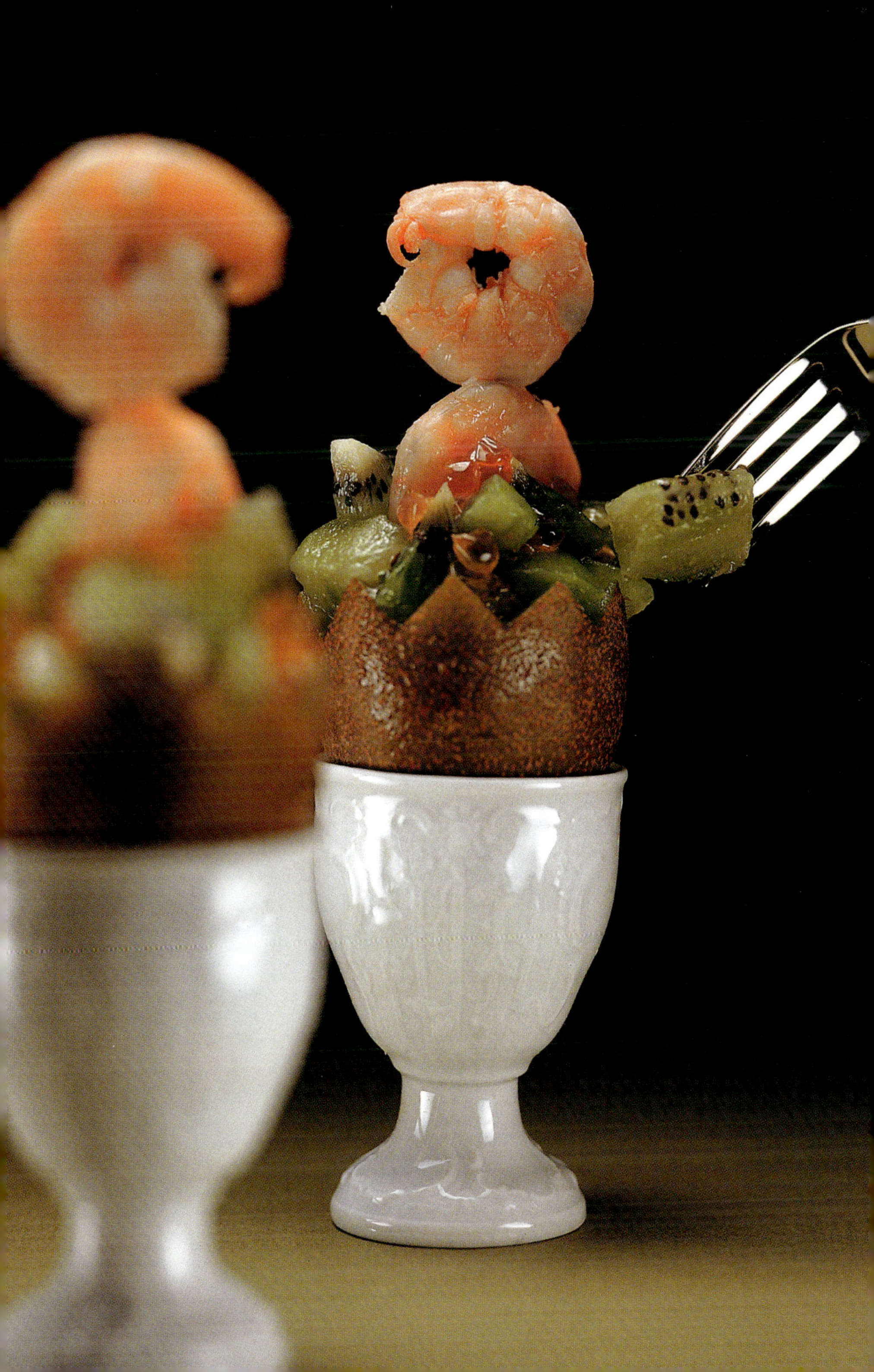

ginger marinated fish

500 g (1 lb) skinned and boned lean white fish or salmon
1 small onion, diced
1 fresh or canned chilli, chopped
2.5 cm (1 in) knob root ginger, grated
1 cup cider or white vinegar
3 ZESPRI™ GREEN Kiwifruit
salt and pepper to taste

Cut the fish in bite-sized chunks. Place into a glass bowl. Combine the onion, chilli, ginger and vinegar and pour over the fish. Marinate in the refrigerator for about 4 hours or until the fish has a cooked appearance. Stir occasionally.

Peel the kiwifruit and cut in 1.5 cm (¾ in) cubes. Drain the fish and combine with the fruit. Season with salt and pepper. **Serves 6.**

antipasto platter

½ cup each: black and green olives, cherry tomatoes
100 g fetta cheese, cubed
8 slices salami
6 smoked mussels
2 ZESPRI™ Kiwifruit

Arrange the olives, tomatoes, cheese, salami and mussels on a large platter. Peel and cube the kiwifruit and add to the platter. Serve with crostini or sliced French bread. **Serves 4-6.**

main courses

Kiwifruit complements a great variety of main course dishes. Meat, fish and poultry all benefit from the addition of this versatile fruit. When kiwifruit is heated it loses some of its attractive bright colour. To retain the colour in hot dishes, add kiwifruit at the end of the cooking, allowing just enough time to warm. When kiwifruit is added to curries or casseroles, it may lose some colour but the tangy flavour is excellent. Kiwifruit can often be used in place of pineapple, apples or oranges in savoury dishes.

meat tenderiser

ZESPRI™ GREEN Kiwifruit contains an enzyme, actinidin, which is an effective meat tenderiser. It is similar to the enzyme papain in pawpaw (papaya). Actinidin breaks down protein. Tough cuts of meat, fish or poultry may be tenderised in two ways:

1. Slice the kiwifruit and place it on top of the meat or fish.
2. First purée or mash the kiwifruit. Fork the meat and paint with the purée. This is the more effective of the two methods. Stand the meat for 30 minutes per 2.5 cm (1 in) of thickness. Do not tenderise for too long as the meat will become mushy. The meat should be wiped dry before grilling or pan-frying.

When tenderising meat prior to casseroling, add the kiwifruit used to the casserole – the heat inactivates the enzyme but the purée will add flavour.

superb steamed mussels

32 green-lipped mussels
4 shallots, diced
2 tablespoons each: balsamic vinegar, orange juice
¼ cup water
3 ZESPRI™ Kiwifruit, peeled and diced
1 tablespoon extra virgin olive oil
freshly ground salt and pepper to taste

Wash the mussels and scrub. Remove any beards. Place in a large saucepan with the shallots, vinegar, orange juice and water. Cover and steam for about 5 minutes, until the shells have just opened. Discard any that do not open.

Place into serving bowls. Strain the cooking liquid and add the oil. Sprinkle the mussels with kiwifruit, strained liquid and salt and pepper. **Serves 4.**

jade prawns

500 g (1 lb) raw prawns (large shrimps)
3-4 tablespoons oil

seasoning: 1 tablespoon grated root ginger
1 teaspoon each: white vinegar, sugar
½ teaspoon salt
2 tablespoons each: tomato sauce (ketchup), water

greens: 1 cup bean sprouts, blanched
4 spring onions (scallions), diagonally sliced
3 ZESPRI™ GREEN Kiwifruit, julienned

Shell the prawns leaving the tails on. De-vein. Heat a wok and bring 2-3 tablespoons of oil to a high heat. Stir-fry the prawns, until the colour changes. Add the seasoning mix and stir-fry for 1 minute, until thick. Remove to one side and keep warm.

In a clean pan, heat the remaining oil and stir-fry the sprouts and spring onions for about 1 minute. Add the kiwifruit and stir-fry for 15 seconds. Serve topped with the prawns. **Serves 4.**

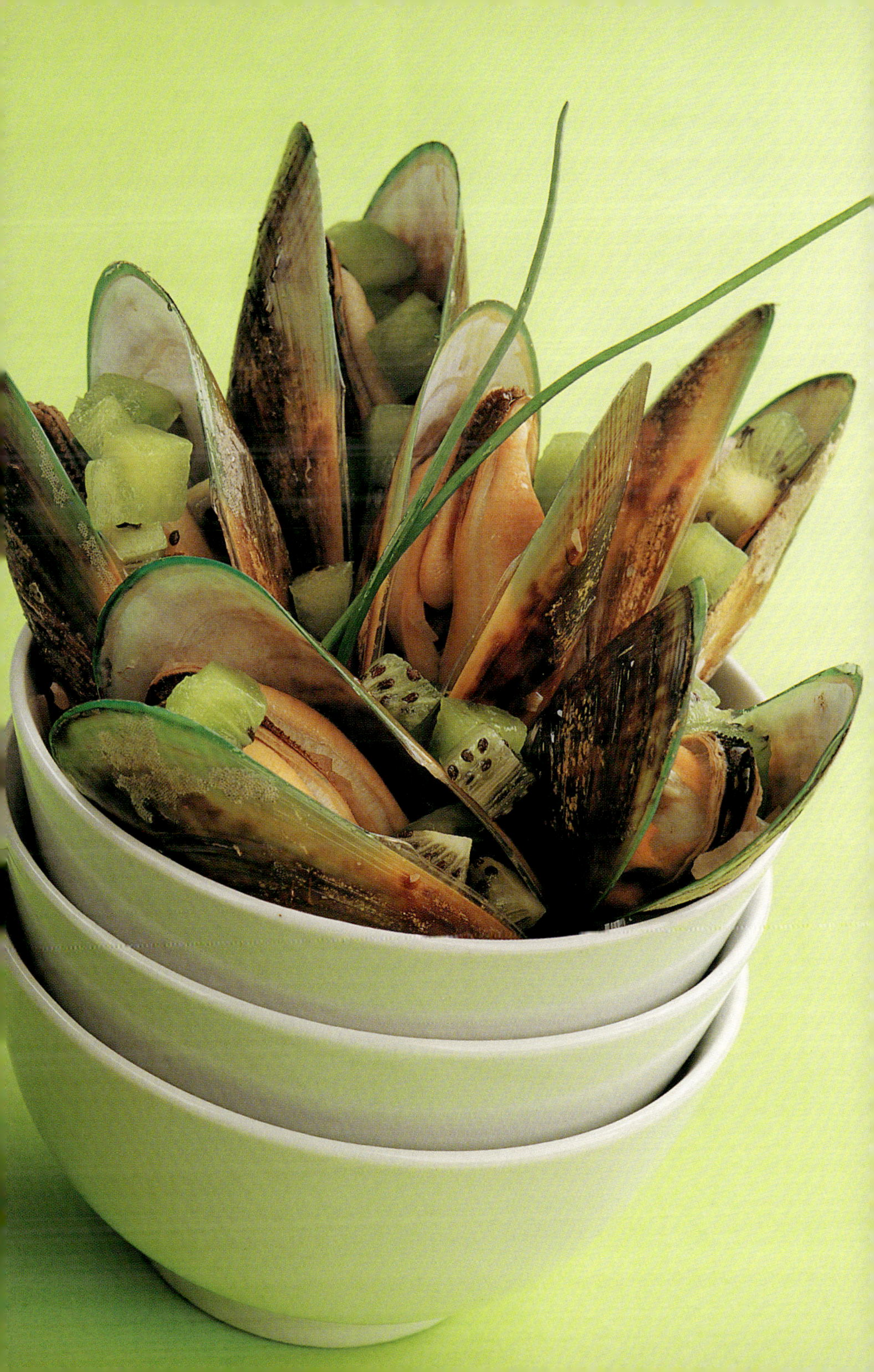

blackened fish with kiwifruit salsa

coating: ¼ *teaspoon salt*
2 teaspoons chilli powder
1 teaspoon paprika
½ teaspoon freshly ground black pepper
¼ teaspoon each: ground cayenne pepper, ground white pepper
1 tablespoon flour

fish: *500 g (1 lb) skinned and boned thick fish fillets*

kiwifruit salsa: *4 ZESPRI™ Kiwifruit*
2 tablespoons finely chopped mint
2-3 shallots, diced
2 cloves garlic, crushed
2 teaspoons white wine vinegar
1 teaspoon sugar
pinch salt
2 teaspoons olive oil, optional

Combine all the ingredients for the coating. Divide the fish in 4 equal portions and sprinkle the coating on both sides.

To prepare the salsa, peel and finely chop the kiwifruit. Combine with all the other ingredients, except the oil.

Heat a non-stick frying pan over high heat. Add the fish and cook for about 2 minutes each side.

Stir the oil into the salsa. Serve with the blackened fish. **Serves 4.**

fish with flair

750 g (1½ lb) skinned and boned lean white fish fillets
salt and pepper to taste
flour
100 g (3½ oz) butter
100 g (3½ oz) cashew nuts
¼ cup orange-flavoured liqueur
juice 2 oranges
2-3 ZESPRI™ Kiwifruit, peeled and sliced

Preheat oven to 150°C (300°F). Divide the fillets in 4 or 5 equal portions. Wipe dry. Dust lightly in seasoned flour.
　In a large, heavy frying pan, melt half the butter over medium heat. Sauté the fish quickly on each side, until just golden. Place on a warm platter in the oven for about 5 minutes while preparing the sauce.
　Melt the remaining butter in the pan. Sauté the cashews, until golden. Pour in the liqueur and flame. Lift out the nuts with a slotted spoon and place to one side. Add the juice to the pan and simmer, until reduced and thick. Meanwhile, top the fish with kiwifruit slices and nuts and warm through in the oven. Pour the sauce over the fish and serve immediately. **Serves 4-5.**

stir-fried squid with kiwi

2 ZESPRI™ GREEN Kiwifruit
300 g cleaned squid (calamari) tubes
2 tablespoons olive oil
3 tablespoons lemon juice
freshly ground salt and pepper to taste
assorted salad leaves or boiled rice

Peel and cut the kiwifruit in half lengthwise then cut the halves in slices.
　Slice the squid in thin rings. Heat the oil in a non-stick frying pan. Stir-fry the squid for 1 minute or until just cooked. Remove from the heat and toss with the lemon juice.
　Carefully combine the kiwifruit with the squid. Season with salt and pepper and serve on a bed of lettuce or rice. **Serves 4.**

balsamic chicken with golden salad

2 skinned and boned, double chicken breasts
2 tablespoons balsamic vinegar
2 cloves garlic, crushed
1 tablespoon each: olive oil, brown sugar
3 ZESPRI™ GOLD Kiwifruit
2-3 cups assorted lettuce leaves

dressing: 2 tablespoons each: balsamic vinegar, extra virgin olive oil
1 teaspoon each: prepared mustard, sugar

Divide the chicken in 4 portions. Combine the vinegar, garlic, olive oil and sugar and pour over the chicken. Marinate for at least 4 hours in the refrigerator.

Peel and slice the kiwifruit. Wash and crisp the lettuce leaves. Arrange on four serving plates. Whisk the ingredients for the dressing.

Cook the chicken under a pre-heated grill for 6-8 minutes each side, depending on thickness. Slice and place on the salad. Drizzle with the dressing. **Serves 4.**

chilli green burrito

1 tablespoon oil
3 cloves garlic, crushed
1 medium onion, chopped
500 g (1 lb) lean minced (ground) chicken or beef
450 g (15 oz) can tomatoes in juice, chopped
1-2 green chillies, seeded and diced
2 ZESPRI™ GREEN Kiwifruit
4 large flour tortillas

Heat the oil and sauté the garlic and onion, until softened. Add the meat and stir until browned, then add the tomatoes and chilli. Cover and cook for about 30 minutes.

Peel and dice the kiwifruit. Warm the tortillas. Spoon the meat mixture onto each tortilla, add some kiwifruit and fold up. Great served with extra kiwifruit, diced tamarillos and sour cream on the side. **Serves 4.**

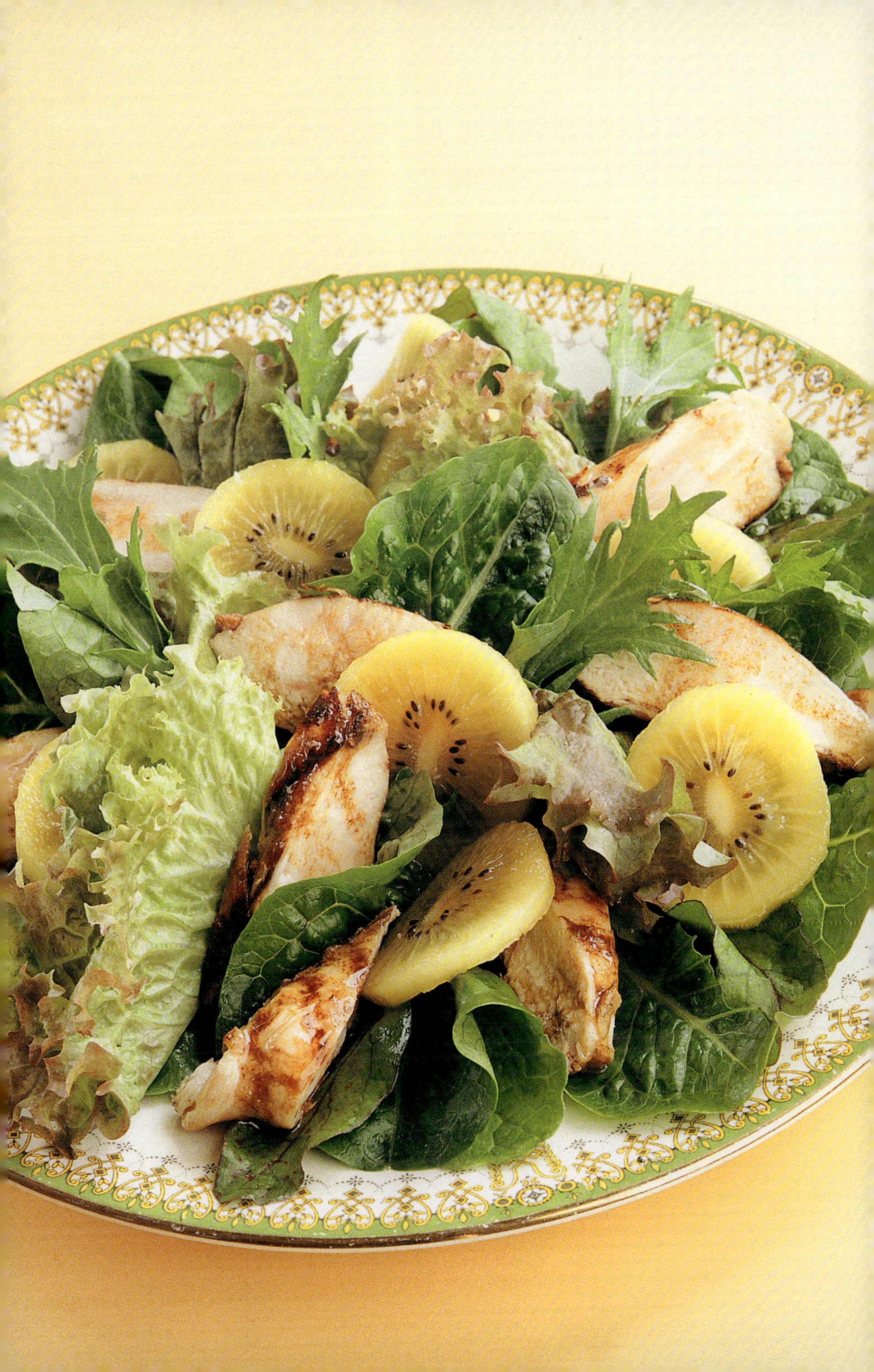

pacific rim chicken

500 g (1 lb) boneless chicken pieces
3 tablespoons each: soy sauce, soy oil, dry sherry
1 tablespoon grated root ginger
1 teaspoon each: grated orange rind, sesame oil
3 ZESPRI™ Kiwifruit
juice 1 orange

Combine the chicken pieces with the soy sauce and oil, sherry, ginger, orange rind and sesame oil. Marinate for at least 4 hours in the refrigerator.
    Peel and slice the kiwifruit.
    Drain the chicken and grill or pan-fry for about 12 minutes or until cooked, turning the chicken often. Add the kiwifruit at the last minute and sprinkle with the orange juice. Great with rice. **Serves 4.**

spicy duck with kiwi

750g (1½ lb) whole roasted duck
1 each: red and yellow peppers (capsicum)
2 tablespoons soy sauce
few drops chilli sauce, to taste
1 tablespoon each: sesame oil, white vinegar, sugar
4 large ZESPRI™ GREEN Kiwifruit
¼ cup pickled ginger

Remove the duck meat from the bones. Cut in strips and place to one side.
    Cut the peppers in 2.5 cm (1 in) squares. Blanch quickly in boiling water, refresh in icy water and pat dry.
    Combine the soy, chilli sauce, sesame oil, vinegar and sugar. Pour over the peppers. Peel and slice the kiwifruit.
    Combine the duck, peppers, kiwifruit and ginger. Serve warm on a bed of rice or at room temperature on watercress. **Serves 4.**

chicken & orange blossom sauce

2 kg (4 lb) chicken portions
¼ cup flour
½ teaspoon salt
spray oil

orange blossom sauce: 1 cup orange juice
2 tablespoons lemon juice
¼ cup brown sugar
1 tablespoon each: soy sauce, cornflour (cornstarch)
3 ZESPRI™ GREEN Kiwifruit, peeled and cut in 1 cm (½ in) cubes
1 tablespoon sesame seeds
orange blossoms, optional

Pre-heat the oven to 180°C (350°F). Shake the chicken portions in a plastic bag with flour and salt – coat well.

Spray a large baking pan with oil. Add the chicken and spray with more oil. Bake for 50 minutes, turning the chicken halfway through cooking.

Meanwhile, make the sauce. Combine the juices, sugar, soy sauce and thickening. Bring to the boil and stir, until thick. Add the kiwifruit and warm through.

Spoon the sauce over the cooked chicken pieces on a serving platter. Sprinkle with sesame seeds and, if using, place the orange blossoms on the side. **Serves 6.**

warm salad of cervena & kiwifruit relish

Cervena is top quality farmed New Zealand venison.

500 g (1 lb) saddle back strap Cervena (venison)
olive oil
freshly ground black pepper to taste

kiwifruit relish: 2 each: ZESPRI™ GREEN and GOLD Kiwifruit
1-2 red chillies, seeded and diced
2 tablespoons chopped coriander (cilantro)
1 tablespoon lemon juice

salad: 4 cups assorted lettuce leaves and sprouts

Brush the venison with the olive oil and sprinkle liberally with black pepper.

Cook under a pre-heated grill for 8-10 minutes each side. Cover and rest for 10 minutes before slicing.

To make the relish, peel and dice the kiwifruit. Combine with the chillies, coriander and lemon juice.

To serve, place the salad greens on four serving plates, top with the sliced warm meat and place the relish on the side. The meat may be topped with a jus or some oyster sauce warmed through with a little jus or orange juice. **Serves 4.**

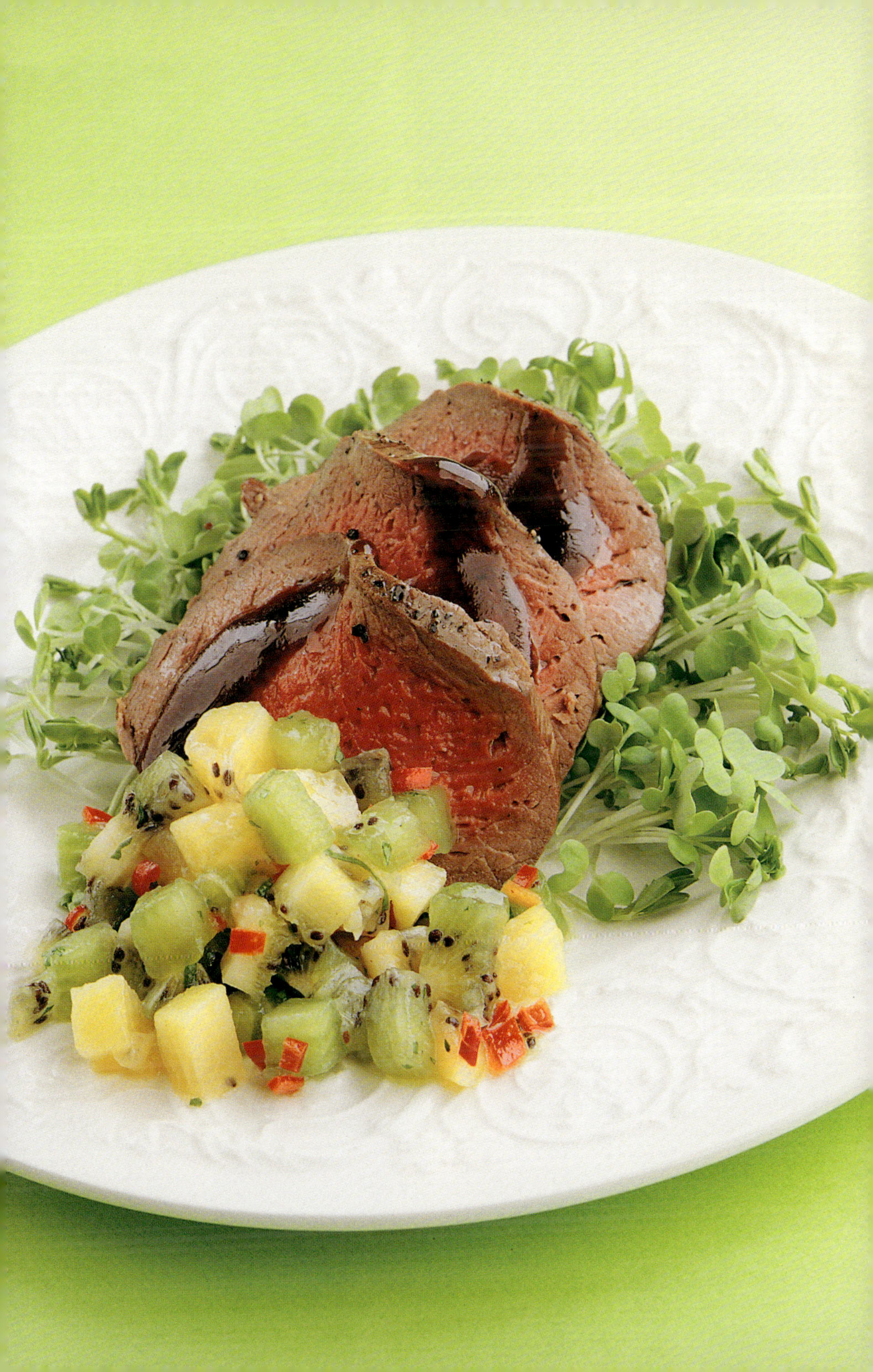

mirin marinated pork

500 g (1 lb) lean pork fillet (tenderloin)
2 tablespoons each: honey, mirin, light soy sauce
3 tablespoons oil
4 firm ZESPRI™ Kiwifruit
1 tablespoon brown sugar

Cut the pork in 2.5 cm (1 in) cubes. Combine the honey, mirin, soy sauce and 1 tablespoon of oil. Mix well. Marinate the meat in this mixture for 1 hour.

Peel the kiwifruit and cut in half crosswise or in quarters if very large. Mix the remaining oil with the brown sugar. Thread the meat and kiwifruit alternately along 4 skewers. Brush the fruit with the oil mixture.

Cook under a pre-heated hot grill (or over a barbecue) for about 4 minutes each side, turning and basting occasionally. Cook, until the meat and fruit is lightly browned. **Serves 4.**

new zealand-style ham steaks

2 ham steaks
2 tablespoons each: butter, brown sugar, orange juice
1 large ZESPRI™ Kiwifruit, peeled and sliced

Pan-fry the ham steaks in the butter for about 1-2 minutes each side. Sprinkle with the brown sugar after turning. Add the orange juice and kiwifruit slices and heat, until just warm. **Serves 2.**

minted lamb skewers

This mint sauce is great with lamb or chicken. The lamb combination also makes great lamburgers.

mint sauce: ¾ cup each: sugar, white vinegar
5 tablespoons water
1 cup packed fresh mint leaves
2 ZESPRI™ Kiwifruit, peeled and sliced

lamb: 500 g (1 lb) minced (ground) lean lamb
2 tablespoons milk powder or 1 small egg
salt and pepper to taste
2 tablespoons finely chopped mint
3 firm ZESPRI™ Kiwifruit, peeled and sliced
oil

To prepare the sauce, heat the sugar in a heavy pan over low heat, until melted. Carefully pour in the vinegar and water. Bring to the boil and simmer for 5 minutes.

Meanwhile, chop the mint in a food processor or blender. Stir into the vinegar mixture. Cool. Add the kiwifruit to the sauce just before serving.

Combine the lamb with the milk powder or egg, salt, pepper and chopped mint. Form into small balls.

Peel the kiwifruit and cut into pieces about the size of the meat balls. Thread onto skewers alternately with the lamb. Brush the skewers with oil and grill for about 3 minutes each side, until just cooked. Great served with a cracked wheat salad or a crisp salad in pocket bread and topped with mint sauce. **Serves 4.**

lamb rack with emerald mint sauce

New Zealand's traditional mint sauce is replaced with an emerald green sauce of kiwifruit and fresh mint.

2 large racks of lamb, about 16 cutlets in total
¼ cup redcurrant jelly

emerald mint sauce: 3-4 ZESPRI™ GREEN Kiwifruit
1 teaspoon each: lemon juice, sugar
4 tablespoons finely chopped fresh mint

Pre-heat the oven to 190°C (370°F). Place the meat in a roasting pan, fat side up. Bake for 20 minutes. Brush regularly with warmed redcurrant jelly. Serve hot or cold.

To prepare the sauce, peel the kiwifruit, mash well or place in a food processor or blender, until just puréed. Stir in the lemon juice, sugar and mint. Serve with hot or cold lamb. Makes 1 cup approximately. **Serves 4.**

lamb noisette hayward

1 boned and rolled loin of lean lamb, about 1.5 kg (3 lb)
3 large ZESPRI™ Kiwifruit
2 teaspoons finely chopped root ginger
1 clove garlic, crushed
2 teaspoons soy sauce
1 tablespoon brown sugar

Pre-heat the oven to 160°C (325 °F). Roll and tie the lamb with string every 4 cm (1½ in).

Peel 1 kiwifruit, mash well and combine with all the other ingredients. Simmer for 1 minute. Place the lamb in an oven dish just large enough to hold it. Bake for 50-60 minutes, basting often with the kiwifruit mixture. Peel and slice the remaining kiwifruit. Place the lamb on a platter, cut into noisettes between each string. Remove the string. Turn, cut face up. Serve hot or cold, topped with sliced kiwifruit. **Serves 5-6.**

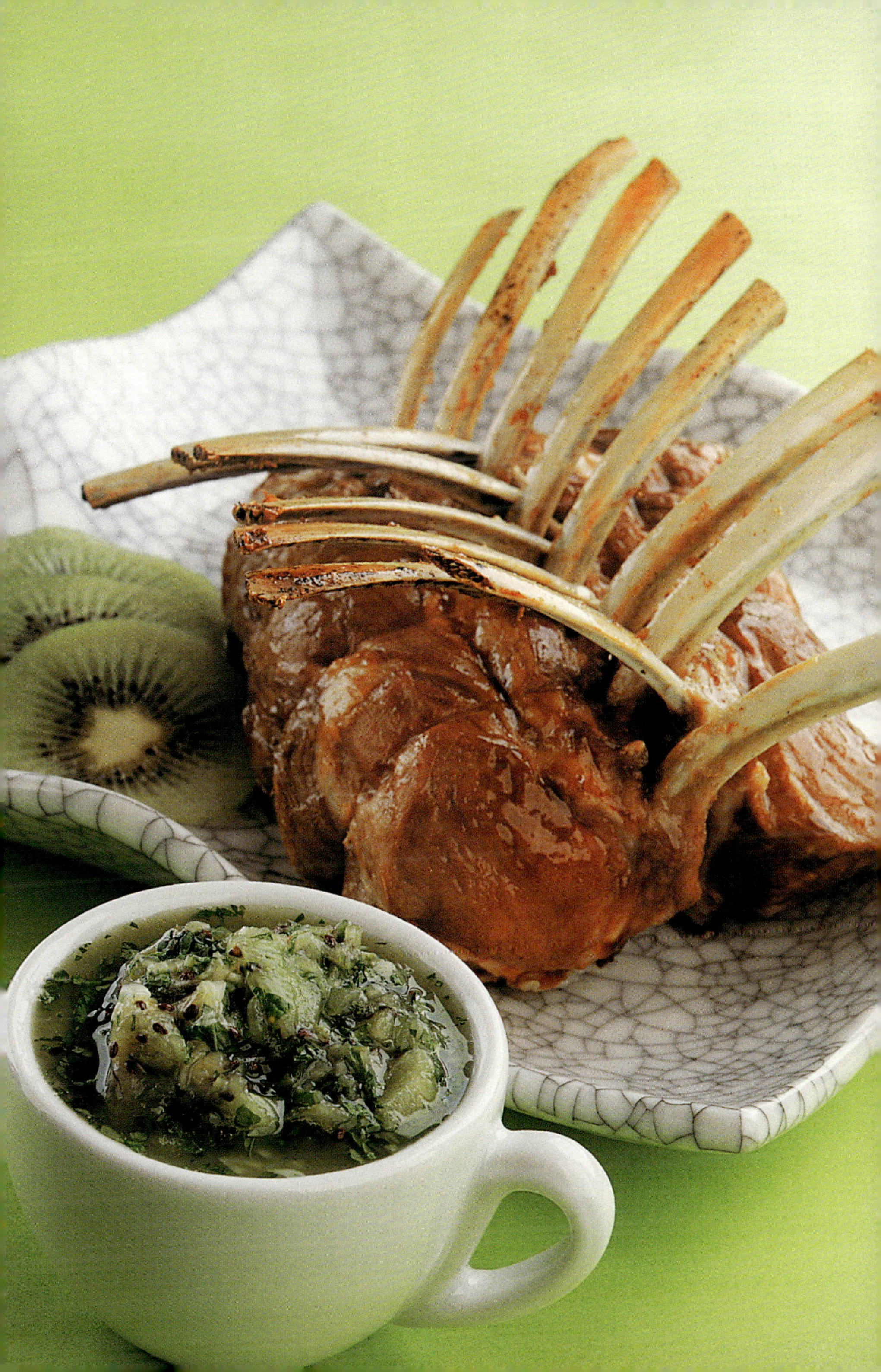

indian beef

750 g (1½ lb) lean stewing beef
2 tablespoons flour
salt and pepper to taste
1 tablespoon curry powder
½ teaspoon mixed spice
2 rashers bacon, diced
2-3 tablespoons ghee or oil
2 tablespoons sugar
grated rind 1 lemon
¼ cup each: water, dry sherry, lemon juice
2 ZESPRI™ Kiwifruit, peeled and sliced

Cut the meat in 2.5 cm (1 in) cubes. Combine the flour and seasonings. Toss the meat in the mixture, firmly pressing it in.

Pan-fry the bacon in the ghee, until crisp. Add the beef a little at a time and pan-fry, until golden on all sides.

Add the sugar, lemon rind, water, sherry, lemon juice and 1 sliced kiwifruit. Cover and simmer on low heat for 2 hours or until tender, adding more water if the curry becomes too dry.

Serve on a bed of rice topped with the remaining kiwifruit. **Serves 6.**

curry accompaniment

Finely diced kiwifruit served plain or mixed with onion, ginger, mustard seeds and yoghurt.

tricolour beef with crispy noodles

400 g (14 oz) frying/grilling steak

marinade: 1 tablespoon each: soy sauce, grated root ginger
2 teaspoons each: cornflour (cornstarch), lemon juice
1 teaspoon sugar

1 each: yellow and red sweet peppers (capsicum)
2 ZESPRI™ GREEN Kiwifruit
3 cloves garlic, crushed
1 tablespoon chilli sauce
3 tablespoons oil
1-2 cups crispy noodles

Cut the beef in thin strips. Combine the ingredients for the marinade, add the beef, stir well and marinate for at least 1 hour.

Seed the peppers and cut in thin strips. Peel and slice the kiwifruit. Place to one side. Combine the garlic and chilli sauce.

Heat the oil in a large wok over high heat. Drain the meat and stir-fry in batches, until coloured. Add the peppers and stir-fry for about 1 minute. Stir in the garlic and chilli until well mixed, then add the kiwifruit. Place the prepared crispy noodles on a serving plate and top with the beef and kiwifruit mixture. **Serves 4.**

bean curd & kiwi

2 cakes firm bean curd (tofu) about 400 g (14 oz)
oil for deep frying
2-3 ZESPRI™ Kiwifruit
4 spring onions (scallions), finely sliced

sauce: *½ cup dark soy sauce*
2 tablespoons palm or brown sugar
3 cloves garlic, crushed

Drain the bean curd and pat dry. Cut the curd in 2.5 cm (1 in) cubes. Heat the oil and deep-fry curd in batches, until browned on all sides. Drain the curd on paper towels then arrange on a serving dish.

Peel the kiwifruit and cut in half lengthwise then slice. Spread over the bean curd. Garnish with the spring onions. Spoon the combined sauce ingredients over and stand for about 1 hour before serving. **Serves 5-6.**

savoury olive crêpes

8 crêpes

filling: *2-3 firm ZESPRI™ GREEN Kiwifruit, peeled and diced*
3 tablespoons finely chopped black olives
150 g (5 oz) Mozzarella cheese, grated
25 g (1 oz) butter

Lay the crêpes out flat and place the kiwifruit on the lower third. Top with a little of the chopped olives and 1-2 tablespoons of cheese and roll up. Repeat with the remaining crêpes and filling.

Pre-heat the oven to 180°C (350°F). Place the crêpes in a baking dish and dot with butter. Loosely cover and heat through in the oven for about 15 minutes, removing the cover for the last few minutes. Can be garnished with fresh herbs. **Serves 4.**

kiwi pizza with pesto

pizza base: 1 tablespoon sugar
1 cup warm water
1½ teaspoons active dried yeast granules
3¼ cups flour
1 teaspoon salt
2 tablespoons olive oil

pesto: 4-6 tablespoons prepared basil pesto

topping: 225 g (8 oz) Mozzarella cheese, sliced
3-4 firm ZESPRI™ GREEN Kiwifruit, sliced
2-3 firm tomatoes, sliced
2-3 tablespoons grated Parmesan cheese
freshly ground black pepper to taste
a few small basil leaves

To prepare the base, dissolve the sugar in the warm water then sprinkle the yeast over. Stir gently. Stand until foamy. Combine the flour and salt in a bowl, make a well in the centre then stir in the yeast mixture and oil. Mix until the dough holds together. Turn the dough onto a lightly floured surface and knead until shiny, about 5 minutes. Allow the dough to rise until doubled in size, punch down then pat out in a thin circle on a lightly greased oven tray.

Pre-heat the oven to 200°C (400°F). Spread the pesto over the pizza base and top with the Mozzarella. Bake for about 15 minutes, until the base is golden.

Remove the pizza from the oven and add the sliced kiwifruit and tomato. Return to the oven for 5 minutes to heat through. Sprinkle with grated Parmesan cheese, pepper and small basil leaves. **Serves 4-6.**

salads

sundried tomatoes & kiwifruit

4 ZESPRI™ Kiwifruit
¼ cup sundried tomatoes, packed in oil
1 tablespoon lemon juice
2 tablespoons chopped basil leaves
freshly ground black pepper

Peel and slice the kiwifruit onto a serving plate. Chop the sundried tomatoes and sprinkle over the kiwifruit with the lemon juice, basil and black pepper. **Serves 4.**

smoked mussel & kiwifruit salad

200 g (7oz) smoked mussels
4 firm ZESPRI™ Kiwifruit, peeled
1 stalk celery, diced
¼ cup vinaigrette (page 40)
freshly ground black pepper
assorted crisp lettuce leaves

Cut the mussels and kiwifruit in 1 cm (½ in) cubes. Combine with the celery in a bowl. Sprinkle with the dressing and black pepper.

Tear the lettuce leaves in medium-sized pieces and place on a serving dish. Top with the mussel mixture.

kiwifruit, sweet pepper & tomato

1 small sweet yellow pepper (capsicum)
1 firm ripe red tomato
2 ZESPRI™ GREEN Kiwifruit
1 tablespoon each: salad oil, white vinegar
½ teaspoon each: French mustard, honey
salt and pepper to taste
3 basil leaves, chopped

Halve and seed the pepper. Cook under a pre-heated grill, until the skin blisters. Place in a plastic bag to cool. Peel the pepper and slice in strips.

Cut the tomato in eighths and discard the seeds. Peel and slice the kiwifruit. Arrange the tomato, pepper and kiwifruit on a small plate.

Whisk the oil, vinegar, mustard and honey, until creamy. Season with salt, pepper and basil and pour evenly over the salad. **Serves 2-4.**

kiwi parmesan

1 crisp green-skinned apple
1 red-skinned apple
2 firm ZESPRI™ GREEN Kiwifruit
¼ cup French dressing
3 tablespoons finely grated Parmesan cheese
freshly ground black pepper to taste
3 tablespoons sliced black olives

Prepare this salad just before serving. Core and thinly slice the apples. Peel and slice the kiwifruit. Place attractively on a flat plate. Sprinkle with the dressing, cheese and black pepper. Top with olives. Excellent with baked chicken. **Serves 3-4.**

salad of brown rice, curry & kiwifruit

1 cup brown rice
1 teaspoon each: garam masala, salt
1 tablespoon curry powder
4 large ZESPRI™ GREEN Kiwifruit, peeled and diced
1 large red-skinned apple, diced
½ cup roasted peanuts

Bring about 2 cups of water to the boil and add the rice, garam masala, salt and curry powder. Simmer until the rice is cooked and the water is absorbed, about 35 minutes.

Cool slightly then add the kiwifruit, apple and nuts. Serve warm or at room temperature. **Serves 4-6.**

scallop salad supreme

10 fresh scallops
1 cup dry white wine
small bunch fresh herbs
1 each: red-skinned apple, small onion, diced
½ cup walnut halves
2 large ZESPRI™ Kiwifruit, peeled and diced
1 tablespoon olive oil
freshly ground salt and black pepper to taste

Place the scallops in a saucepan with the wine. Add the herbs and slowly bring to boiling point. Poach for 5 minutes, until tender. Drain and slice.

Just before serving, combine the apple, onion, walnuts and kiwifruit. Sprinkle with olive oil and season with salt and pepper. Excellent served on a bed of spinach leaves. **Serves 4.**

spicy thai fruit salad

salad: 2 large ZESPRI™ Kiwifruit
1 cup each: black and green seedless grapes, lychees
½ cup each: cubed pawpaw (papaya), watermelon balls, sliced water chestnuts
1 red-skinned apple, sliced

dressing: 3 tablespoons lime juice
1 teaspoon each: salt, sugar

topping: 2-3 tablespoons oil
3 cloves garlic, sliced
3 shallots, sliced
½ cup cooked prawns (shrimps)
lettuce leaves

garnish: 1-2 chillies, seeded and sliced

Peel the kiwifruit, cut in quarters lengthwise, then cut in wedges. Place in a bowl with the other fruits. To make the dressing, mix the lime juice, salt and sugar then pour over the fruit.

Meanwhile, heat the oil in a small frypan. Fry the garlic and shallots separately, until crisp but not brown. Drain on paper towels.

Place the lettuce leaves on a serving plate, spoon the fruit and dressing over attractively and top with the prawns, garlic and shallots. Garnish with the chillies. **Serves about 6.**

fruit salad with chilli oil

4 ZESPRI™ GREEN Kiwifruit
½ small pawpaw (papaya)
1 teaspoon minced chilli
3 tablespoons each: oil, finely chopped coriander (cilantro)

Peel and slice the kiwifruit. Peel the pawpaw and remove the seeds. Cut the flesh in small pieces. Combine with the kiwifruit in a bowl. Mix the chilli and oil and sprinkle over the fruit just before serving. Sprinkle with the coriander. **Serves 4-6.**

avocado green & gold with soy dressing

2 avocados
2 each: ZESPRI™ GREEN and GOLD Kiwifruit
1 tablespoon julienned root ginger
freshly ground back pepper to taste

soy dressing: 1 clove garlic, crushed
1 teaspoon grated root ginger
¼ teaspoon finely diced chilli
2 tablespoons each: soy sauce, salad oil
1 tablespoon lemon juice

Halve the avocados and remove the stones. Peel and slice the kiwifruit and place in the centre of the avocados. Sprinkle with the julienned root ginger and pepper.

Whisk all the ingredients for the dressing and spoon over the fruit just before serving. **Serves 4.**

kiwifruit vinaigrette

2 ZESPRI™ Kiwifruit
½ cup fruit vinegar
1 tablespoon liquid honey
1 teaspoon smooth, prepared mustard
¼ teaspoon salt
¼ cup mild olive oil or salad oil

Peel the kiwifruit and purée. Whisk the vinegar, honey, mustard and salt in a bowl and add the kiwifruit. Slowly whisk in the oil. Chill before serving. **Makes about 1 cup.**

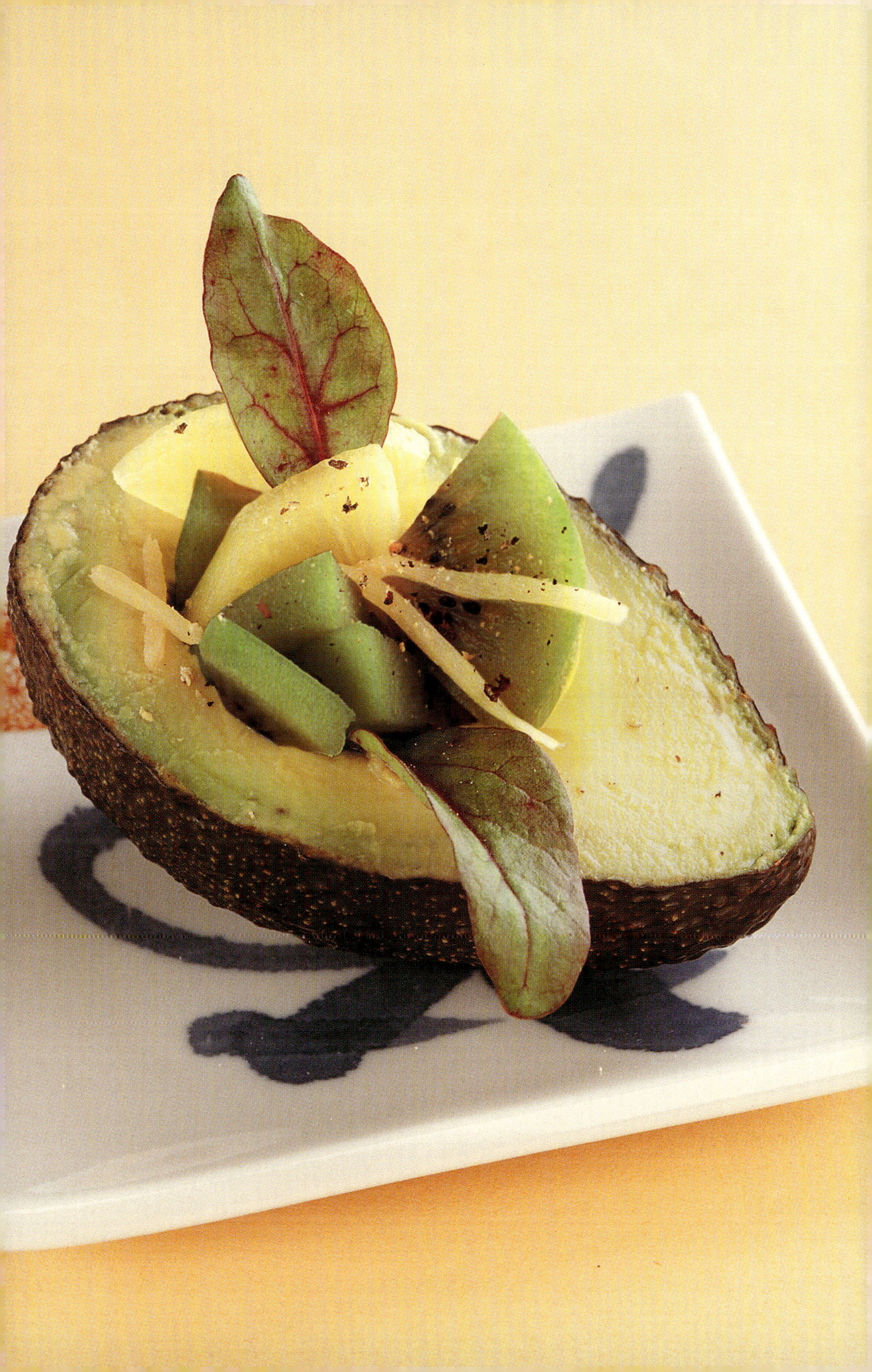

sweet treats

Kiwifruit is ideal for providing glamorous endings to dinners. Simple but delicious desserts can be made by just slicing the fruit, sprinkling it with sugar and adding your favourite liqueur. Kiwifruit use is limited only by imagination.

Actinidin, the enzyme in ZESPRI™ GREEN Kiwifruit which tenderises meat by breaking down protein, can also cause gelatine to break down. The fruit must first be cooked to inactivate the enzyme. Agar-agar – a vegetable setting agent not affected by the enzyme – is available from health and oriental food stores and can be used as a substitute for gelatine in kiwifruit jellies.

Powdered agar-agar looks like powdered gelatine – use ¼ of a teaspoon to set 1 cup of liquid. When cooked, kiwifruit has a 'gooseberry-like' flavour which is excellent where flavour is of the utmost importance such as in pies and puddings.

fruit salads & platters

Kiwifruit combines well with everyday and exotic fruits to provide memorable salads. Serve in bowls or arrange attractively on platters.

tropical salad

juice 2 oranges
1 tablespoon each: liquorice-flavoured liqueur, sugar
1 cup canned lychees
½ pawpaw (papaya)
4-5 ZESPRI™ Kiwifruit

Combine the orange juice, liqueur and sugar and stir, until dissolved.
    Drain the lychees. Peel, seed and cube or slice the pawpaw. Peel and slice the kiwifruit.
    Arrange the fruit attractively on a platter or place in a salad bowl. Pour the orange juice mixture over the fruit. Nuts such as almonds, brazil nuts or hazelnuts can also be added. **Serves 8.**

Other combinations – ZESPRI™ Kiwifruit with:
finely grated orange rind and orange-flavoured liqueur
sliced oranges, preserved ginger and fruit liqueur
strawberries and walnuts
tamarillos and honey
passionfruit pulp

melon with kiwifruit coulis

1 rock melon (cantaloupe)
200 g (7 oz) watermelon
5 large ZESPRI™ GREEN Kiwifruit
1-2 tablespoons caster (powdered/superfine) sugar
1 tablespoon lemon juice
herbs or flowers for garnishing

Quarter the rock melon, remove the seeds, peel and slice in wedges.
    Prepare balls from watermelon using a melon baller. Peel one kiwifruit and make some kiwifruit balls.
    Peel the remaining kiwifruit and purée carefully in a food processor or blender, then sieve. Add sugar and lemon juice to taste. Spoon the kiwifruit coulis onto four serving plates. Fan slices of melon on the coulis and top with watermelon and kiwifruit balls. Garnish with herbs or flowers. **Serves 4.**

pavlova

The Pavlova, New Zealand's national dessert, is a crisp shell of meringue with a marshmallow centre, topped with whipped cream and fruit.

pavlova: *2 egg whites*
1½ cups caster (powdered/superfine) sugar
½ teaspoon vanilla essence (extract)
1 teaspoon each: cornflour (cornstarch), white vinegar
4 tablespoons boiling water

topping: *1¼ cups cream*
1 tablespoon icing sugar (confectioners') sugar
2-3 ZESPRI™ Kiwifruit

Pre-heat the oven to 180°C (350°F). Place all the ingredients for the Pavlova into a large mixing bowl. Beat with a rotary beater or electric beater until the mixture is smooth, shiny and stiff, about 12 minutes.

Meanwhile, place a sheet of greaseproof paper on a baking tray. Brush lightly with the melted butter or oil and sprinkle with the cornflour (cornstarch). Shake off the excess.

Spoon the meringue mixture onto the prepared tray, forming a 23 cm (9 in) circle.

Bake in the middle of the oven for 10 minutes, then reduce the heat to 150°C (300°F) and bake for a further 45 minutes. Cool in the oven.

To serve, whip the cream with the icing sugar, until stiff. Spread on top of the cold Pavlova.

Peel and slice the kiwifruit. Purée some for a sauce. Top the Pavlova with the sliced kiwifruit and spoon some of the purée over, just before serving. **Serves about 6.**

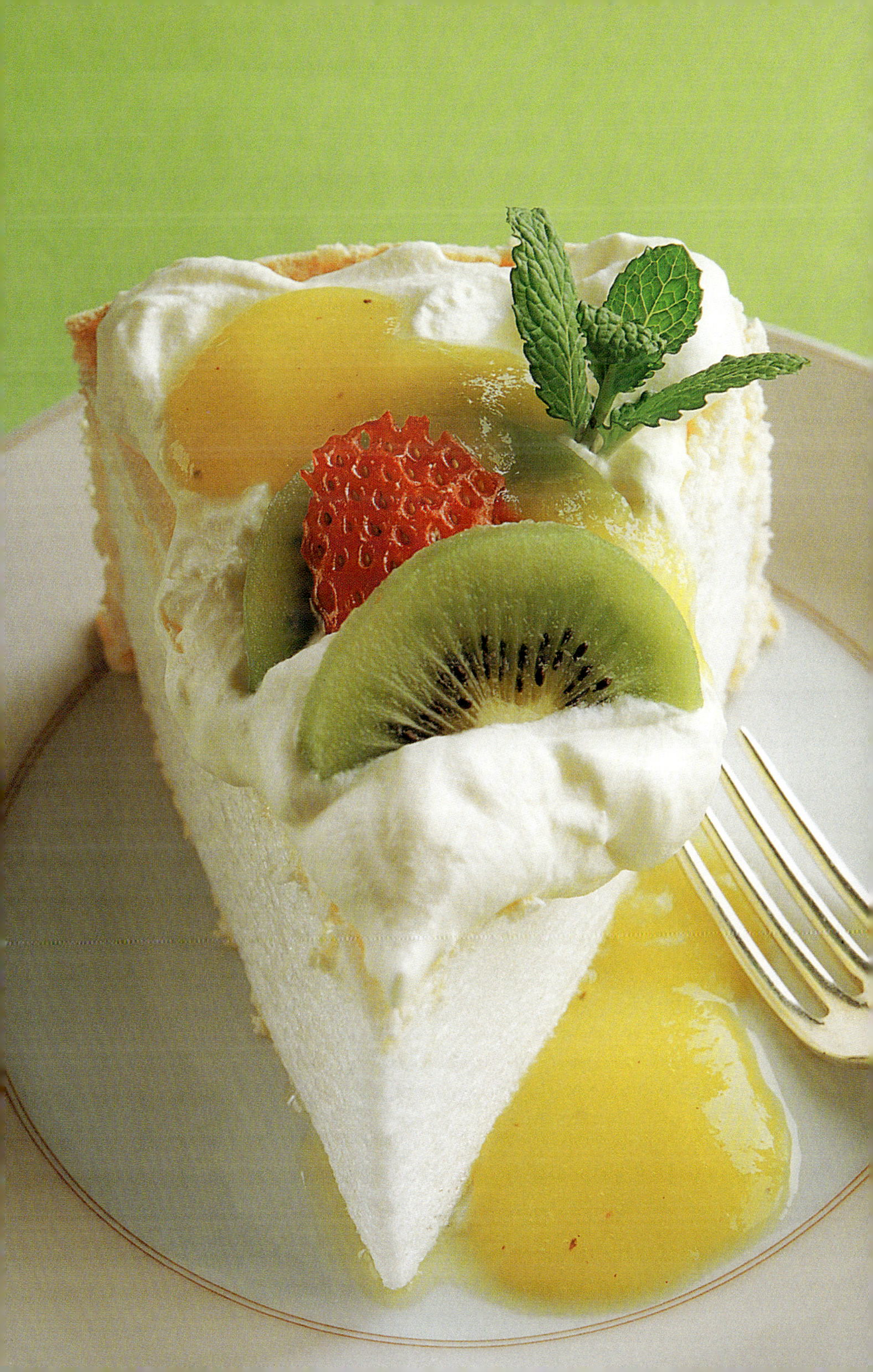

glazed fruit flan

The filling can also be used in individual tartlets.

1 baked 20-23 cm (8-9 in) flan shell

filling: *2 cups cultured sour cream or similar*
¼ cup icing (confectioners') sugar
finely grated rind ½ orange
2 teaspoons orange juice
1 teaspoon vanilla essence (extract)
2-3 ZESPRI™ Kiwifruit
1 cup grapes
3 tablespoons sieved apricot jam

Place the flan on a serving plate. Beat the sour cream and the icing sugar, until smooth. Add the rind, juice and vanilla.

Spoon into the prepared flan shell and smooth the top. Chill. Peel and slice the kiwifruit. Arrange with the grapes in an attractive pattern on top of the filling. Warm the apricot jam and brush over the fruit. **Serves 6-8.**

kiwifruit meringue pies

6 x 10 cm (4 in) baked pastry tart shells or
12 baked tartlet shells
4-5 ZESPRI™ Kiwifruit
6 teaspoons sugar

topping: *2 egg whites*
¼ cup caster (powdered/superfine) sugar

Pre-heat the oven to 200°C (400°F). Place the prepared tart or tartlet shells on an oven tray. Peel and slice the kiwifruit and place on the base of the tarts or tartlets. Sprinkle with a little sugar.

Beat the egg whites, until frothy. Add the caster sugar and continue beating, until stiff and shiny. Spoon or pipe over the kiwifruit. Bake for about 4 minutes, until the meringue is golden. Alternatively, cook under a medium-heat grill, until golden. **Serves 6.**

tiramisu

3 ZESPRI™ Kiwifruit
3 egg yolks
½ cup icing (confectioners') sugar
¼ cup Tia Maria liqueur
250 g (9 oz) cream cheese
1¼ cups cream
200 g (7 oz) lady (sponge) fingers
1¼ cups strong coffee
1 tablespoon cocoa

Peel and the slice the kiwifruit. Line the sides of eight individual clear glass dishes or wine glasses with slices of kiwifruit. Beat the egg yolks, icing sugar and liqueur over hot water, until light. Cool.

Beat the cream cheese and add to the egg yolk mixture. Dip the lady fingers into the coffee to just moisten. Place a layer of the fingers into each serving dish. Spoon the cheese mixture over the top, add more lady fingers and more cream cheese mixture. Chill in the refrigerator. Sprinkle with cocoa just before serving. Alternatively, this dessert can be made in one large bowl. **Serves 8.**

fruit sushi

1 cup short grain rice
2 cups coconut cream
2 tablespoons sugar
4 ZESPRI™ Kiwifruit
6 strawberries
½ cup passionfruit pulp, optional

Wash the rice well then soak in cold water for 1 hour. Bring the coconut cream and the sugar to the boil. Drain the rice and slowly stir into the coconut cream mixture. Bring to the boil, reduce the heat, cover and cook until all the liquid is absorbed by the rice. Stir occasionally. Spoon into a square dish and pat into a block about 2.5 cm (1 in) thick. Cool, then refrigerate.

Meanwhile, prepare the fruit, peel and slice half of the kiwifruit. Make balls or cubes from the remainder. Hull and slice the strawberries. Cut the rice in rounds using a biscuit cutter. Arrange the fruit on top. Serve with the passionfruit pulp on the side if desired. **Serves 6.** *(Photograph page 2.)*

timbales with scarlet sauce

1½ cups sweet white wine or clear apple juice
1½ teaspoons powdered agar-agar
4 large ZESPRI™ Kiwifruit
2 tablespoons finely diced crystallised ginger

sauce: 1 cup raspberries, puréed and sieved
2 ZESPRI™ Kiwifruit, puréed and sieved
sugar to sweeten, optional

accompaniment: fresh raspberries, melon or kiwifruit balls

Simmer the wine for about 5 minutes then remove from the heat. Slowly add the agar-agar, stirring well. Boil for about 5 minutes, until the agar-agar is dissolved. Cool.

Peel the kiwifruit and dice. Mix with the ginger. Divide the mixture evenly into four moulds then pour in the jelly and allow to set.

To serve, spoon a little of each purée onto four serving plates. Unmould jellies onto each plate. Garnish with fruit. **Serves 4.**

sugared kiwifruit with coconut cream

6 large ZESPRI™ Kiwifruit
3 tablespoons palm or brown sugar
1 cup coconut cream

Peel the kiwifruit and slice. Sprinkle with half the sugar. Refrigerate. Dissolve the remaining sugar in the coconut cream. Chill. Spoon over the kiwifruit when serving. **Serves 4-5.**

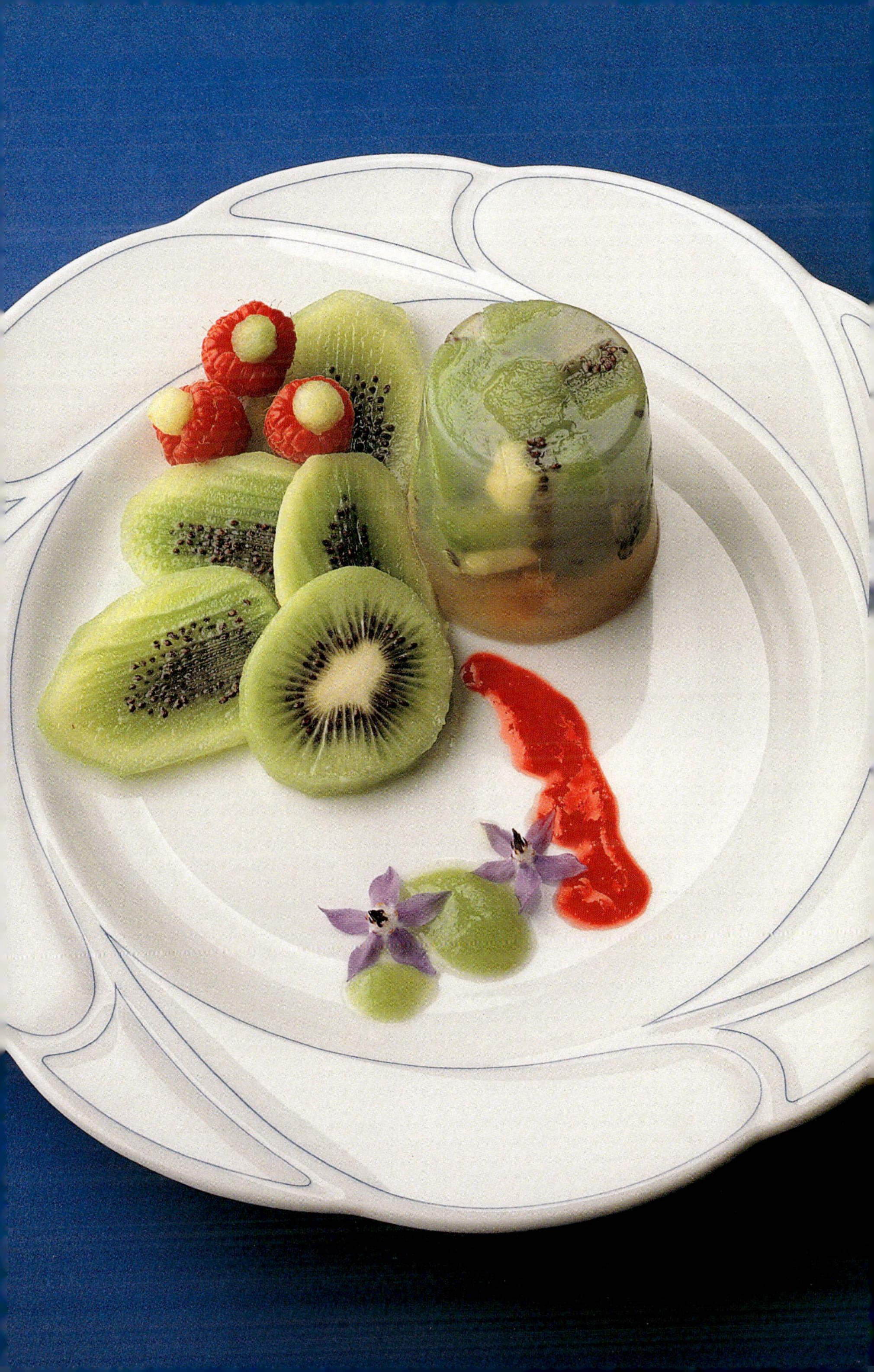

stir-fried kiwifruit with lychees

4 ZESPRI™ Kiwifruit
500 g (1 lb) can lychees
1 tablespoon butter or margarine
1 tablespoon each: lemon and orange juices, sugar
2 tablespoons brandy

Peel the kiwifruit and cut in chunks. Drain the lychees and place on a platter with the kiwifruit. Melt the butter over medium heat in a wok or chafing pan. Add the fruit and stir-fry for 1 minute. Add the fruit juices and sugar and stir-fry for another minute. Add the warmed brandy then flame. Serve immediately with whipped cream or ice cream. **Serves 4.**

kiwifruit mousse

4 large ZESPRI™ Kiwifruit
finely grated rind and juice 1 orange, 1 lemon
½ cup sugar
3 teaspoons powdered gelatine
2 tablespoons water
4 egg whites
1 cup cream, whipped

Mash the kiwifruit and sieve. Place in the top of a double boiler with the rind, fruit juices and half the sugar. Stir briskly over hot water, until the sugar is dissolved. Remove from heat and cool.

Soak the gelatine in cold water then dissolve over low heat. Add to the fruit mixture and leave until just beginning to set. Whip the egg whites with remaining sugar, until stiff and shiny. Fold into the fruit with whipped cream. Pour into individual dishes or one attractive serving dish. Refrigerate to chill. **Serves 6.**

kiwiana yoghurt

See the recipe for Kiwi Sauce on page 55.

2 bananas
1 cup plain yoghurt
2 tablespoons cream
1 tablespoon sugar
½ cup Kiwi Sauce
2 egg whites

Mash the bananas coarsely and combine with the yoghurt, cream and sugar. Fold in the kiwifruit sauce. Whip the egg whites until stiff and fold into the yoghurt mixture. Spoon into serving dishes. **Serves 4.**

fillo triangles

Slices of kiwifruit wrapped in paper-thin, Greek-style fillo pastry and baked or deep-fried, until crisp.

4 sheets fillo pastry
3-4 ZESPRI™ Kiwifruit, peeled
4-5 tablespoons safflower oil
oil for deep frying, optional
caster (powdered/superfine) sugar

Use one sheet of fillo at a time. Cut each sheet into 8 cm (3 in) wide strips. Brush each strip with a little oil. Slice the kiwifruit in 5 mm (¼ in) rounds.

Place one kiwifruit slice on the end of each fillo strip. Take a corner of the fillo and fold it over to form a triangle, covering the kiwifruit.

Lift the first triangle up and over to form a second triangle. Continue folding over and over until the end of the pastry strip is reached. When all pastry triangles have been prepared lower, a few at a time, into deep, hot oil. Fry until golden – drain well. Alternatively, brush with oil and bake in a hot oven. Serve sprinkled with caster sugar. **Makes 16 triangles.**

light green & gold cheesecake

base and sides: 75 g (3 oz) butter, melted
1 cup biscuit crumbs
¼ cup icing (confectioners') sugar
1 each: ZESPRI™ GREEN and GOLD Kiwifruit

filling: 3 eggs, separated
½ cup sugar
250g (9 oz) each: ricotta cheese, cream cheese
2 ZESPRI™ GOLD Kiwifruit, peeled and mashed
1 cup cream, whipped

topping: extra ZESPRI™ Kiwifruit

Lightly grease a loose-based 23 cm (9 in) cake pan. Prepare the crust by combining the crushed biscuits, icing sugar and butter. Mix well. Press into the base of the pan. Peel and slice the kiwifruit and stand in a single row around the inside of the pan.

To prepare the filling, place the egg yolks and sugar in the top of a double boiler and whisk over boiling water, until thick and creamy. Cool.

Beat the cheeses, until well blended. Add the cooled egg mixture and mix well. Fold the mashed kiwifruit into the cheese mixture with the whipped cream. Beat the egg whites to the soft peak stage. Fold into the cheese mixture. Pour into the prepared pan, cover and freeze, until firm.

To serve, remove the cheesecake from the freezer and stand at room temperature to soften slightly – about 15 minutes. Garnish with extra peeled and diced kiwifruit. Alternatively, remove slices of the cheesecake as required and return the remainder to the freezer. **Serves 8-10.**

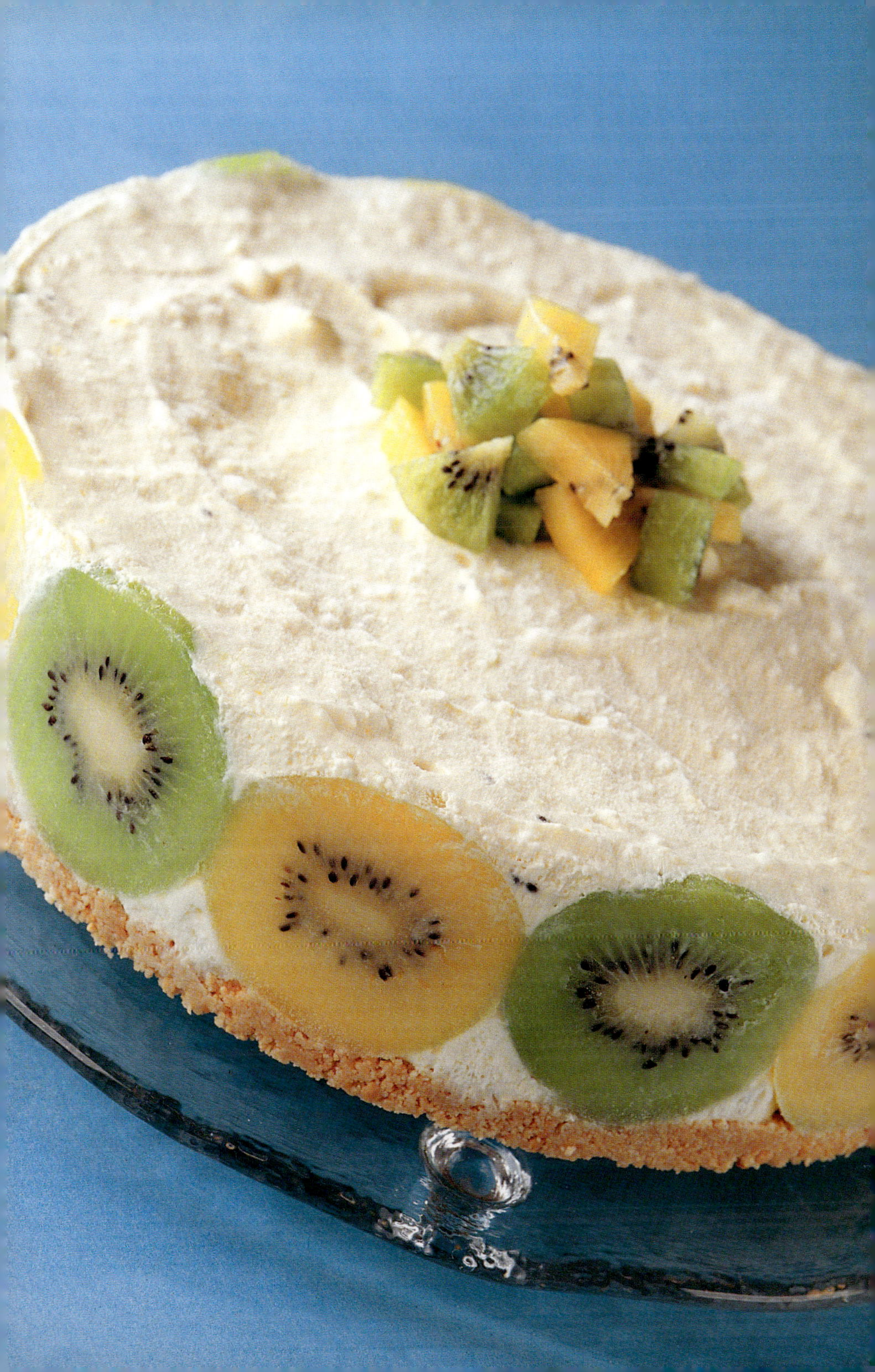

kiwifruit waffles

2 cups flour
1 teaspoon baking powder
2 eggs, lightly beaten
1½ cups milk
2 tablespoons each: oil, raw sugar
2 ZESPRI™ Kiwifruit

Sift the flour and baking powder into a bowl. Gradually stir in the combined eggs, milk, oil and sugar until smooth. Peel and dice the kiwifruit and add to the batter.

Pour about 4 tablespoons of the mixture onto hot waffle irons and cook, until golden. Repeat. Excellent served with peeled and sliced kiwifruit and whipped cream or yoghurt. Alternatively, serve with Kiwifruit Jam – see page 63.

pancakes with apricots, almonds & kiwifruit

12 prepared pancakes or crêpes

filling: *½ cup sieved apricot jam*
finely grated rind and juice 1 lemon
¼ cup chopped, toasted almonds
1 banana, diced
2-3 ZESPRI™ Kiwifruit, peeled and diced
icing (confectioners') sugar

Warm the pancakes slightly, either on a plate over hot water or in the microwave.

Heat the jam, rind, lemon juice and nuts. Add the fruit and gently heat through – do not allow the kiwifruit to change colour. Spoon a little of the mixture onto each pancake and fold over.

Place two on each serving plate and dust with icing sugar. Excellent served with whipped cream. **Serves 6.**

kiwi gelato with pistachio nuts

3-4 ZESPRI™ Kiwifruit
75 g (3 oz) shelled pistachio nuts
½ cup sugar
1 teaspoon vanilla essence
¾ cup milk

Peel and slice the kiwifruit. Mash and sieve, or process in a food processor, until well mashed. Sieve if desired. Grind the nuts finely.

Combine the sugar and kiwifruit with vanilla, milk and nuts. Freeze in an ice cream maker preferably, or in the deep freeze, until almost solid. Beat well then return to the freezer, until solid. Thaw in the refrigerator for about 10 minutes before serving. **Serves 4-5.**

kiwi sauce

This sauce is delicious over ice cream or as a topping for cheesecakes or raw fruit. It may be frozen.

3-4 ZESPRI™ Kiwifruit
3-4 teaspoons caster (powdered/superfine) sugar or sugar syrup
1-2 teaspoons lemon juice

Pulp the kiwifruit by mashing well with a fork or placing in a food processor or blender for a short time. Sieve.

Do not over-process the fruit – the crushed seeds make the sauce taste bitter and give it a speckly appearance.

Add the sugar or sugar syrup and a dash of lemon juice. **Makes about 1 cup.**

kiwifruit ice cream

6 large ZESPRI™ Kiwifruit
150 g (5 oz) caster (powdered/superfine) sugar
3 eggs, separated
1¼ cups cream, whipped

Peel and mash the kiwifruit – leave some pieces lumpy. Stir in half the sugar and stand for 15 minutes.
    Beat the egg yolks and remaining sugar over hot water, until thick and creamy. Cool. Beat the whites, until stiff. Fold the yolks then the whites into the fruit together with the whipped cream. Freeze quickly.
    Store in an airtight container in the coldest part of the freezer. **Serves about 6.**

kiwifruit sorbet

¾ cup sugar
2 cups water
finely grated rind and juice 1 lemon
6 large ZESPRI™ Kiwifruit

Dissolve the sugar in water then add the rind and juice. Boil steadily for 10 minutes. Chill.
    Peel, mash and sieve the kiwifruit. There should be about 2 cups of pulp. Combine the pulp with equal amounts of cold sugar syrup. Place in the freezer in a suitable container and freeze, until mushy. Beat well then freeze, until stiff. **Serves 6-8.**

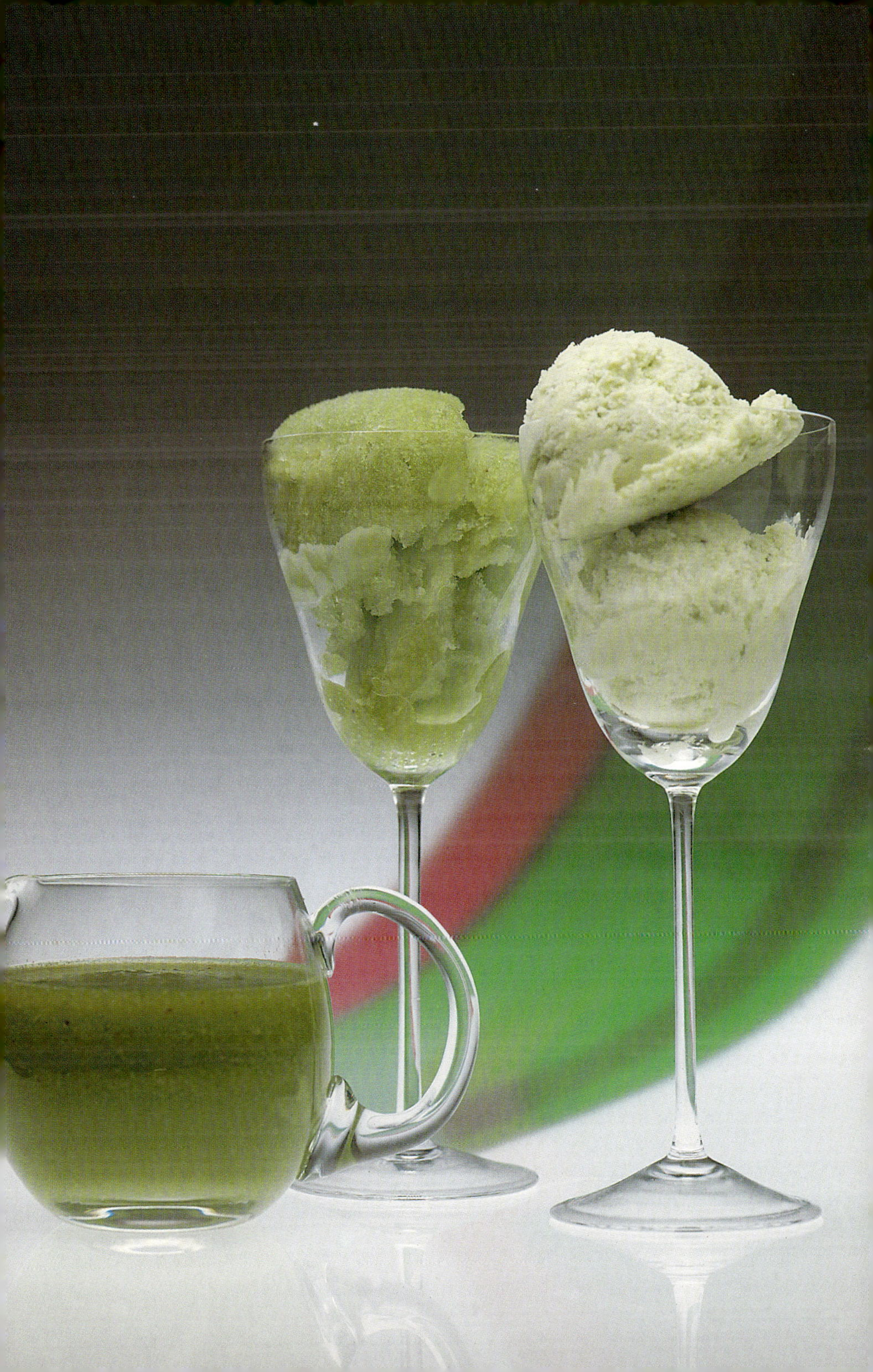

baked kiwifruit with nut topping

4 large ZESPRI™ Kiwifruit
2 tablespoons brown sugar
2 tablespoons apricot jam or orange marmalade

topping: 50 g (2 oz) butter, chilled
¾ cup flour
2 tablespoons sugar
½ cup each: mixed blanched almonds, walnuts, coarsely chopped
2 tablespoons sherry
½ cup cream, whipped
nutmeg to taste

Pre-heat the oven to 190°C (375°F). Peel and slice the kiwifruit into a baking dish. Sprinkle with brown sugar and dot with jam.

To make the topping, rub the butter into the flour with fingertips. Add the sugar and nuts. Spread over the fruit.

Bake for 20 minutes. Sprinkle with sherry and serve hot with whipped cream flavoured with a dash of nutmeg. **Serves 4-5.**

kiwi madeira

A cake with sliced kiwifruit reminiscent of apple cake.

200 g (7 oz) butter
1 cup sugar
3 eggs
1 cup self-raising flour
½ cup cornflour (cornstarch)
2 thinly sliced ZESPRI™ Kiwifruit

Pre-heat the oven to 180°C (350°F). Lightly grease and line the base of a 20 cm (8 in) square cake pan.

Cream the butter and sugar, until light. Add the eggs one at a time, beating well after each addition. Sift in the flour and cornflour and mix well. Add the kiwifruit. Pour the cake mixture into the prepared pan. Bake for 50 minutes. Turn off the oven and leave the cake (in the oven) for a further 20 minutes. Can be served warm, but also keeps well in a cool place.

kiwi muffins

¼ cup sugar
2 cups flour
2½ teaspoons each: baking powder, custard powder
1 egg, lightly beaten
½ cup milk
100 g (3½ oz) butter, melted
3 ZESPRI™ Kiwifruit, peeled and diced

Pre-heat oven to 200°C (400°F). Lightly grease 8-10 muffin pans.
　Place the sugar, sifted flour and baking powder and custard powder into a bowl. Combine the egg, milk and melted butter. Add the liquid ingredients and diced kiwifruit to the dry ingredients and combine quickly, until just moistened.
　Spoon into the muffin pans. Bake for 20-25 minutes depending on size. **Makes 8-10.**

kiwifruit bread

A moist loaf – excellent with coffee.

¼ cup each: liquid honey, mild-flavoured oil
1 egg
1½ cups wholemeal flour
¼ teaspoon each: salt, ground cloves
1 teaspoon each: cinnamon, baking powder
1 cup each: raisins, chopped nuts
3 large ZESPRI™ Kiwifruit

Pre-heat the oven to 180°C (350°F). Lightly oil a 20 x 13 cm (8 x 5 in) loaf pan.
　Beat the honey, oil and egg well. Sift the flour, salt, spices and baking powder into the oil mixture. Lightly stir in the remaining ingredients. Spoon into the prepared loaf pan. Bake for 40-45 minutes. Cool before slicing. May be spread with butter or margarine when served.

hazelnut meringue cake

Layers of hazelnut meringue sandwiched with liqueur-flavoured cream and kiwifruit.

75 g (3 oz) hazelnuts
3 egg whites
¾ cup caster (powdered/superfine) sugar

filling: 4-5 ZESPRI™ Kiwifruit
1¼ cups cream
1 tablespoon each: icing (confectioners') sugar, orange-flavoured liqueur

Toast the hazelnuts under a hot grill for 3-4 minutes. Rub with a clean cloth to remove the skins. Place the nuts in a food processor or blender and chop very finely. Pre-heat the oven to 150°C (300°F).

Beat the egg whites until stiff, add half the sugar and beat until smooth. Carefully fold in the remaining sugar and hazelnuts.

Cover one or two baking trays with non-stick baking paper (or prepare as for a Pavlova tray). Make three even circles of meringue mixture, about 18 cm (7 in) in diameter. (One circle may have to be cooked on another tray).

Bake for 45-55 minutes or until dry and crisp. The layers may be stored in an airtight container, until required.

To prepare the filling, peel the kiwifruit, halve lengthwise and slice across. Whip the cream and sugar until stiff, fold in the liqueur. Spread a ¼ of the cream on the first layer of meringue. Add a few slices of kiwifruit. Top with another layer of meringue, spread with more cream and fruit. Cover with the top layer of meringue, spread with remaining cream and decorate with kiwifruit slices. **Serves 8.**

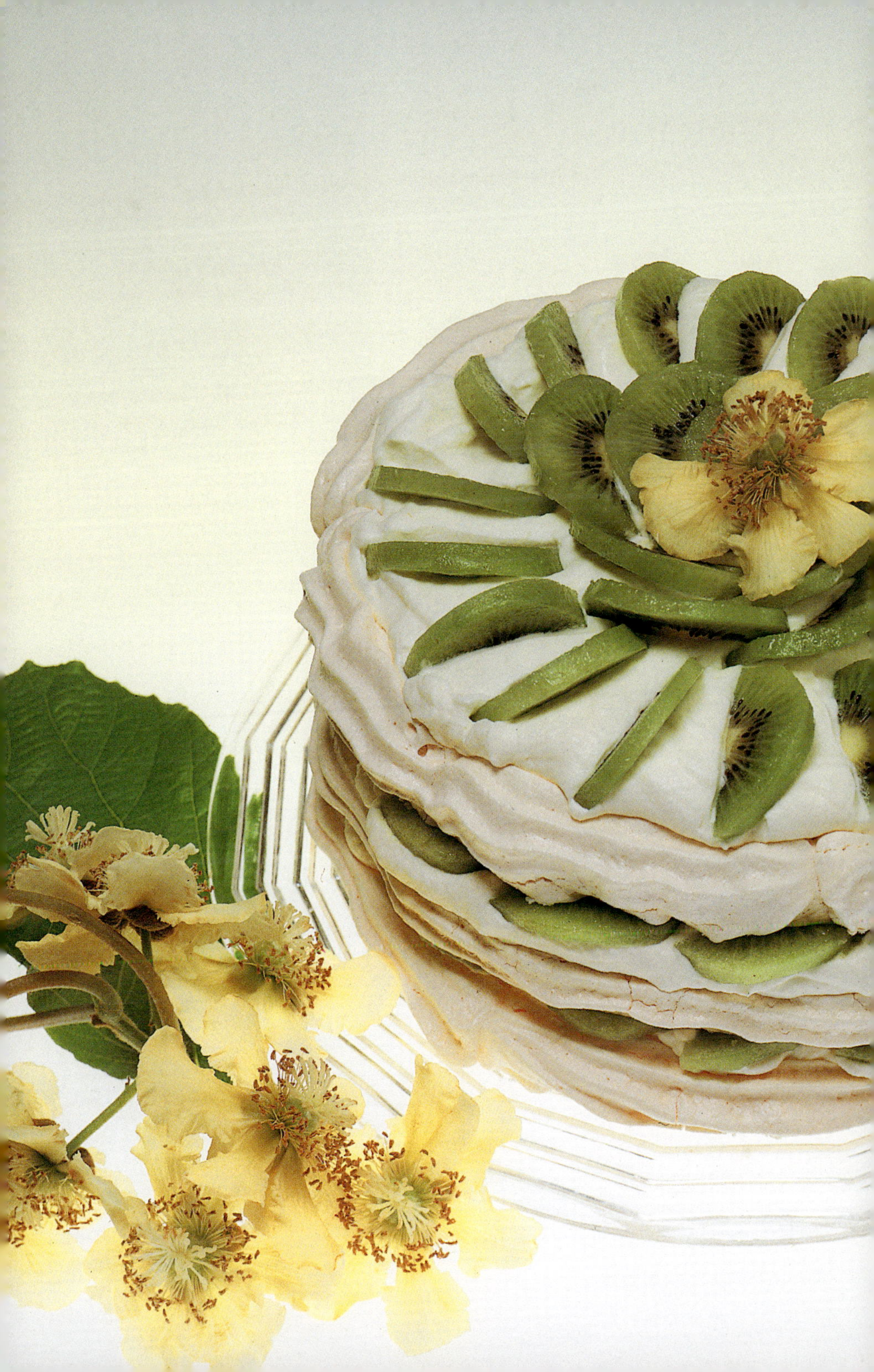

preserves

freezing

Choose firm, mature kiwifruit for freezing. Peel and thickly slice.
Add 1 tablespoon of lemon juice per cup of fruit to retain the colour.
 There are several methods by which kiwifruit can be prepared for freezing:

- **free-flow freezing**

Place a single layer of thickly-sliced kiwifruit on a tray lined with waxed paper. Cover and freeze. Once frozen, the slices can be removed from the tray and stored in the freezer in an airtight bag. To use, remove the kiwifruit from the freezer five minutes before they are required. Or thaw in the refrigerator for about 15 minutes. Use immediately in salads or cakes.

- **freezing in syrup**

Place kiwifruit slices in a container and cover with a medium syrup (2 parts water, 1 part sugar). Freeze. To use, thaw and use in desserts.

- **freezing with sugar**

Thickly slice the kiwifruit and combine with sugar – 1 part sugar to 4 parts fruit. Store in an airtight container in the deep freeze. To use, thaw and serve as a dessert with cream or use in hot pies and puddings.

- **freezing as pulp**

To each cup of pulped kiwifruit add 1 tablespoon of lemon juice and 1 tablespoon of sugar. The pulp may be sieved to remove seeds. Use the thawed pulp in drinks and as a topping for flans, cakes or ice cream.

- **freezing whole**

Do not peel the kiwifruit but rub off any excess fuzz. Place in a plastic bag then seal and freeze. To use, peel and cook – from a frozen state – in savoury casseroles or cooked desserts.

kiwifruit freezer jam

Liquid pectin can be substituted for powdered pectin. Use according to the instructions on the bottle.

3 cups peeled, mashed ZESPRI™ kiwifruit (about 10)
¼ cup lemon juice
5¼ cups sugar
¾ cup water
1 packet (45g/1¾ oz) powdered fruit pectin

In a bowl, combine the kiwifruit, lemon juice and sugar. Stir to blend thoroughly. Stand for 30 minutes. Meanwhile, mix the water and pectin in a small saucepan. Bring to a full boil for 1 minute, stirring constantly. Stir into the kiwifruit mixture all at once. Continue stirring for 3 minutes.

Ladle immediately into sterilised jars, leaving 1 cm (½ in) space at the top. Wipe clean with a damp towel. Cover with lids. Stand at room temperature for 24 hours, then store in the freezer. This jam will keep in the refrigerator for up to three weeks. **Makes about 7 cups.**

microwave kiwifruit jam

500 g (1 lb) ZESPRI™ Kiwifruit
juice 1 lemon
2 cups sugar

Peel the kiwifruit and slice in 5 mm (¼ in) rounds. Place into a large microwave-proof bowl with the lemon and sugar. Add the squeezed lemon halves.

Bring to the boil in the microwave, about 2 minutes. Stir carefully to dissolve the sugar. Boil for about 15 minutes, until setting point is reached 104°C (220°F). Remove the lemon halves. Pour the jam into hot, clean jars. Cover. **Makes about 2 cups.**

kiwifruit & lychee jam

1 kg (2 lb) ZESPRI™ Kiwifruit, peeled and pulped
juice 1 lemon
¼ cup water
4 cups sugar
500 g (1 lb) can lychees, drained

Place the pulp in a saucepan with the lemon juice and water. Tie the lemon peel and pips in muslin and add to the pan. Slowly bring to boiling point, stirring occasionally. Simmer until the fruit has softened. Add the sugar and stir, until dissolved. Add the halved lychees and boil briskly, until setting point is reached 104°C (220°F). Pour into hot, clean jars and seal. **Makes about 6 cups.**

kiwifruit vinegar infused with lavender

500 g (1 lb) ZESPRI™ Kiwifruit
2 cups white wine vinegar
¾ cup sugar
green food colouring, optional
4 sprigs English lavender

Peel and slice the kiwifruit into a large glass bowl. Add the vinegar. Cover and stand for two days in a cool place. Stir occasionally.

Strain well, reserving the liquid. Discard the kiwifruit. Add the sugar to the liquid with food colouring (if using) and lavender. Boil for 8 minutes then strain into sterilised bottles. Add a few lavender leaves to the bottles.

Use the vinegar as a base for salad dressings or sauces or add a little to a cup of water and drink as an alternative to tea. **Makes 2½ cups.**

KIWIFRUIT REFRIGERATOR RELISH
KIWIFRUIT VINEGAR INFUSED WITH LAVENDER
KIWIFRUIT LYCHEE JAM

kiwi refrigerator relish

½ cup shallots
1 medium sweet red pepper (capsicum)
½ cup sliced white radish
1 cup each: sugar, white vinegar
¼ cup water
1 teaspoon each: mustard seeds, black peppercorns
4-5 firm ZESPRI™ Kiwifruit
¼ cup fresh mint leaves

Peel the shallots, seed the pepper and cut in 1 cm (½ in) squares. Bring a large saucepan of water to the boil. Add the shallots, pepper and radish. Remove from the heat and stand for 2 minutes. Drain and refresh in icy water.
  When cold, drain and pat dry. Stand to air-dry for 2 hours.
  Meanwhile, bring the sugar, vinegar, water, mustard seeds and peppercorns to the boil. Cool.
  Peel and slice the kiwifruit. Place all relish ingredients including the mint in a sterilised jar. Cover with the pickling solution. Seal and store in the refrigerator for five days before using. **Makes about 2½ cups.**

traditional kiwifruit chutney

2 onions, chopped
2 cloves garlic, crushed
1 tablespoon finely grated root ginger
1 cup each: brown sugar, cider vinegar
½ cup sultanas
750 g (1½ lb) ZESPRI™ Kiwifruit, peeled and sliced

Place the onions, garlic, ginger, sugar, vinegar and sultanas into a large, heavy saucepan and bring to the boil. Simmer for 30 minutes or until the mixture thickens. Add the kiwifruit and simmer for about 20 minutes, until thick. Pour into hot, sterilised jars, filling to the top. Seal when cold. **Makes about 4 cups.**

mango & kiwifruit chutney

1 cup cider vinegar
1½ cups sugar
1 teaspoon grated root ginger
1 clove garlic, crushed
1 cinnamon stick
½ cup sultanas
425 g can (15 oz) can mangoes, drained
500 g (1 lb) ZESPRI™ Kiwifruit

Combine the vinegar and sugar in a heavy saucepan and bring to the boil. Add the ginger, garlic, cinnamon stick and sultanas and cook for 2 minutes. Continue cooking until the liquid is reduced by about half. Cut the mangoes in 2 cm (¾ in) pieces.

    Remove the cinnamon stick from the pan then add the mangoes and kiwifruit pulp. Return to the boil and simmer, until thick. Pour into hot sterilised jars and seal. **Makes about 3 cups.**

sauternes or red wine preserved kiwifruit

2 cups sauternes or good red wine
½-1 cup sugar
1 kg (2 lb) ZESPRI™ Kiwifruit

Add a ½ cup of sugar to the sauternes or 1 cup of sugar to the red wine. Heat, stirring until the sugar is dissolved. Simmer for 5 minutes. Peel the kiwifruit and cut in half lengthwise. Place in hot, clean jars and cover with the hot wine syrup to within 1 cm (½ in) of the top. Either, seal and process in a waterbath for 20 minutes, or place the jars in the centre of the oven on a wad of newspaper. Cover, and cook at 150°C (300°F) for 30 minutes. Remove the jars and top with vacuum seals.

nutrition

ZESPRI™ Kiwifruit is not only juicy and delicious, but incredibly nutritious.

Research carried out by leading food scientists in the United States shows that the humble kiwifruit is a nutritional powerhouse that aids in the fight against many chronic illnesses, assists digestion and may even help us feel happier and less stressed.

Are you careful about what you eat? ZESPRI™ Kiwifruit provides good fibre and is packed with beneficial nutrients. Everyone appreciates a little extra energy and it does wonders for pregnant women, adolescents, growing children and overworked parents.

Here are just some of the benefits of ZESPRI™ Kiwifruit:

- ZESPRI™ Kiwifruit is a great aid for digestion, containing a property that acts like a laxative.
- ZESPRI™ Kiwifruit contains antioxidants. Antioxidants attack free radicals which damage vital cells.
- A fruit for men? Yes – ZESPRI™ Kiwifruit contains lutein which has been linked to the prevention of prostate cancer.
- Go natural. Have higher energy levels with ZESPRI™ Kiwifruit – a great source of potent carbohydrates, vitamins (B group) and antioxidants (vitamins C and E).
- ZESPRI™ Kiwifruit has a very high level of vitamin C which helps with wound healing.
- A rejuvenator? Yes – ZESPRI™ Kiwifruit contains vitamin E which is beneficial if you are feeling stressed, physically or mentally.
- ZESPRI™ Kiwifruit is full of natural goodness, including folate. Folic acid is part of our DNA, making new cells to replace old or damaged ones. Folic acid has also been found to assist in preventing heart disease.

Whether you have a refreshing, tangy ZESPRI™ GREEN Kiwifruit, a sweet, juicy luscious ZESPRI™ GOLD Kiwifruit or both – you'll be receiving essential nutrients you and your family need to enjoy a healthy daily lifestyle.

Photograph page 69 courtesy of ZESPRI International Ltd.

kitchen help

Recipes in this book use standard level measurements. For successful cooking use either metric weights or measures, or imperial weights and measures – do not mix the two.

In many recipes, American/imperial equivalents of metric measures are shown in brackets. Although the metric yield of a cup is about 10% greater, the proportions remain the same.

abbreviations

metric
g   grams
kg kilograms
mm millimetre
cm centimetre
ml millilitre
°C degree Celsius

american/imperial
in inch
lb pound
oz ounce

cups & spoon measures

(to nearest round number)

	metric	american/imperial
¼ cup	60 ml	2 fl oz
½ cup	125 ml	4 fl oz/¼ pint
1 cup	250 ml	9 fl oz/½ pint
2 cups	500 ml	1 pint (American)
4 cups	1000 ml or 1 litre	1 quart
1 teaspoon	5 ml	
1 desertspoon	10 ml	
1 tablespoon	15 ml	½ fl oz
2 teaspoon	1 dessertspoon	
3 teaspoon	1 tablespoon	
16 tablespoon	1 cup	

alternative names

In the English speaking world, many culinary terms and names of foods cross national borders without creating confusion. However, some may need explanation.

cake tin	cake/baking pan	hard-boiled egg	hard cooked egg
peppers	capsicums/sweet peppers	icing sugar	confectioners' sugar
caster sugar	fine granulated sugar, superfine sugar	minced meat	ground meat
		pawpaw	papaya
coriander	cilantro, Chinese parsley	flour	plain flour/ all purpose flour
cornflour	cornstarch	tomato sauce	ketchup
essence	extract	tomato purée	tomato sauce (USA)
eggplant	aubergine	rockmelon	cantaloupe
frying pan	skillet	sieve	strain
grill	broil	spring onions	scallions, green onions
green prawns	raw prawns or shrimps	seed	pit

index

antipasto platter 16
avocado green & gold with soy dressing 40
baked kiwifruit with nut topping 58
balsamic chicken with golden salad 22
bean curd & kiwi 34
blackened fish with kiwifruit salsa 20
chicken & orange blossom sauce ... 25
chilli green burrito 22
curry accompaniment 32
emerald mint sauce 30
fillo triangles 51
fish with flair 21
freezing 62
fruit refresher 6
fruit salad with chilli oil 39
fruit salads & platters 42
fruit sushi 47
ginger & kiwifruit cocktail 8
ginger marinated fish 16
glazed fruit flan 46

hazelnut meringue cake 60
indian beef 32
jade prawns 18
kiwi colada 8
kiwi gelato with pistachio nuts ... 55
kiwi madeira 58
kiwi orange soup 12
kiwi parmesan 37
kiwi pizza with pesto 35
kiwi sauce 55
kiwiana yoghurt 51
kiwiberry cooler 8
kiwifruit & caviar 14
kiwifruit & grapefruit sorbet 14
kiwifruit & lychee jam 64
kiwifruit bread 59
kiwifruit freezer jam 63
kiwifruit ice cream 56
kiwifruit meringue pies 46
kiwifruit mousse 50
kiwifruit muffins 59
kiwifruit refrigerator relish 66

kiwifruit relish	26
kiwifruit salsa	20
kiwifruit sorbet	56
kiwifruit vinaigrette	40
kiwifruit vinegar infused with lavender	64
kiwifruit waffles	54
kiwifruit, sweet pepper & tomato	37
lamb noisette hayward	30
lamb rack with emerald mint sauce	30
light green & gold cheesecake	52
ma ho	12
mango & kiwifruit chutney	67
meat tenderiser	17
melon with kiwifruit coulis	43
microwave kiwifruit jam	63
minted lamb skewers	29
mirin marinated pork	28
new zealand-style ham steaks	28
open sandwiches	10
pacific rim chicken	24
pancakes with apricots, almonds & kiwifruit	54
pavlova	44
rolled sushi with kiwifruit	9
salad of brown rice, curry & kiwifruit	38
sauternes or red wine preserved kiwifruit	67
savoury olive crêpes	34
scallop salad supreme	38
smoked mussel & kiwifruit salad	36
spicy duck with kiwi	24
spicy thai fruit salad	39
stir-fried kiwifruit with lychees	50
stir-fried squid with kiwifruit	21
sugared kiwifruit with coconut cream	48
sundried tomatoes & kiwifruit	36
superb steamed mussels	18
timbales with scarlet sauce	48
tiramisu	47
traditional kiwifruit chutney	66
tricolour beef with crispy noodles	33
tropical salad	43
warm salad of cervena & kiwifruit relish	26
whitebait & kiwifruit roulade	13
yoghurt whip	6